Cultures and Societies in a Changing World

Sociology for a New Century

A PINE FORGE PRESS SERIES

Edited by Charles Ragin, Wendy Griswold, and Larry Griffin

Sociology for a New Century brings the best current scholarship to today's students in a series of short texts authored by leaders of a new generation of social scientists. Each book addresses its subject from a comparative, historical, global perspective, and, in doing so, connects social science to the wider concerns of students seeking to make sense of our dramatically changing world.

- *How Societies Change* Daniel Chirot
- *Cultures and Societies in a Changing World* Wendy Griswold
- *Crime and Disrepute* John Hagan
- *Constructing Social Research* Charles C. Ragin
- *Women and Men at Work* Barbara Reskin and Irene Padavic
- *Cities in a World Economy* Saskia Sassen

Forthcoming Titles

Social Psychology and Social Institutions Denise and William Bielby

Global Transitions: Emerging Patterns of Inequality
York Bradshaw and Michael Wallace

Schools and Societies Steven Brint

The Social Ecology of Natural Resources and Development
Stephen G. Bunker

Ethnic Dynamics in the Modern World Stephen Cornell

The Sociology of Childhood William A. Corsaro

Racism and the Modern World Wilmot James

Gods in the Global Village Lester Kurtz

Waves of Democracy John Markoff

A Global View of Development Philip McMichael

Health and Society Bernice Pescosolido

Organizations in a World Economy Walter W. Powell

Cultures and Societies
in a Changing World

Wendy Griswold
The University of Chicago

PINE FORGE PRESS
Thousand Oaks ◆ London ◆ New Delhi

Copyright © 1994 by Pine Forge Press

For information, address:

Pine Forge Press
A Sage Publications Company
2455 Teller Road
Thousand Oaks, California 91320
(805) 499-4224
Internet: sdr@pfp.sagepub.com

Administrative Assistant: Chiara Huddleston
Editor: Janet Brown
Production Editor: Diane S. Foster
Designer: Lisa S. Mirski
Typesetter: Joseph Cribben
Cover: Lisa S. Mirski
Print Buyer: Anna Chin
Printer: Malloy Lithographing, Inc.

Printed in the United States of America

94 95 96 97 98 10 9 8 7 6 5 4 3 2 1

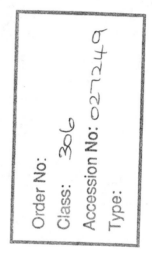

Order No:
Class: 306
Accession No: 027249
Type:

Library of Congress Cataloging-in-Publication Data

Griswold, Wendy.
   Cultures and societies in a changing world / Wendy Griswold.
      p. cm. — (Sociology for a new century)
   Includes bibliographical references (pp. 157-163) and index.
   ISBN 0-8039-9018-9 (pb : acid-free paper)
      1. Culture. 2. Social change. I. Title. II. Series.
HM101.G832   1994
306—dc20   93-44571

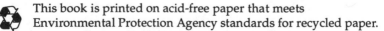

Contents

Figures

ABOUT THE AUTHOR

Wendy Griswold has a background in both social science and the humanities. She received her Ph.D. in Sociology from Harvard University in 1980 and has an M.A. in English from Duke University. Since 1981 she has taught at the University of Chicago, where she holds a joint appointment in Sociology and the Committee on the History of Culture. She has been associate editor and book review editor of the *American Journal of Sociology* and consulting editor of *Contemporary Sociology*. She has received research support from the National Science Foundation, the National Endowment for the Humanities, and the Center for Advanced Studies in the Behavioral Sciences, where she was a Fellow in 1990-1991.

Her research on culture has been international in scope. Her first book was on the English theater (*Renaissance Revivals: City Comedy and Revenge Tragedy in the London Theatre 1576-1980* [University of Chicago Press, 1986]). Other published research has treated American and British nineteenth-century novels; the reception of a Barbadian author in the West Indies, Great Britain, and the United States; and the social context of contemporary Nigerian literature. Currently, she is studying cultural regionalism in the United States and Norway. In addition, she has coedited a book on the sociology of literature (*Literature and Social Practice* [University of Chicago Press, 1989]) and has written on the sociology of religion, specifically conflict within churches. She also has written a paper on sociological methods for cultural analysis ("A Methodological Framework for the Sociology of Culture," *Sociological Methodology* 17 [1987]: 1-35), which has been the basis for numerous lectures and didactic seminars at the American Sociological Association; much of her methodological thinking is incorporated in the present book.

ABOUT THE PUBLISHER

Pine Forge Press is a new educational publisher, dedicated to publishing innovative books and software throughout the social sciences. On this and any other of our publications, we welcome your comments, ideas, and suggestions. Please call or write to:

Pine Forge Press
A Sage Publications Company
2455 Teller Road
Thousand Oaks, CA 91320
(805) 499-4224
Internet:sdr@pfp.sagepub.com

Foreword

Sociology for a New Century offers the best of current sociological thinking to today's students. The goal of the series is to prepare students, and—in the long run—the informed public, for a world that has changed dramatically in the last three decades and one that continues to astonish.

These goals reflect important changes that have taken place in sociology. The discipline has become broader in orientation, with an ever growing interest in research that is comparative, historical, or transnational in orientation. Sociologists are less focused on "American" society as the pinnacle of human achievement and more sensitive to global processes and trends. They also have become less insulated from surrounding social forces. In the 1970s and 1980s sociologists were so obsessed with constructing a science of society that they saw impenetrability as a sign of success. Today, there is a greater effort to connect sociology to the ongoing concerns and experiences of the informed public.

Each book in this series offers a comparative, historical, transnational, or global perspective in some way, to help broaden students' vision. Students need to be sensitized to diversity in today's world and to the sources of diversity. Knowledge of diversity challenges the limitations of conventional ways of thinking about social life. At the same time, students need to be sensitized to the fact that issues that may seem specifically "American" (for example, the women's movement, an aging population bringing a strained social security and health care system, racial conflict, national chauvinism, and so on) are shared by many other countries. Awareness of commonalities undercuts the tendency to view social issues and questions in narrowly American terms and encourages students to seek out the experiences of others for the lessons they offer. Finally, students also need to be sensitized to phenomena that transcend national boundaries—trends and processes that are supranational (for example, environmental degradation). Recognition of global processes stimulates student awareness of causal forces that transcend national boundaries, economies, and politics.

Reflecting the dramatic increase in global cultural interaction, *Cultures and Societies in a Changing World* explores the complex interplay between culture—idea systems, artworks, popular culture, religious beliefs, common sense—and social structure. Within the framework of the "cultural diamond" this book uses a comparative analysis of cultural objects and practices in Nigeria, China, the United States, and other locations around the world to demonstrate how cultural producers and consumers express a changing world through culture and how culture itself contributes to social changes. Chapter-long examinations of the culture construction of social problems and of organizational transactions reveal how the application of a culturally informed approach can illuminate seemingly noncultural issues ranging from those involving social justice to those entailed in practical business operations.

Preface

Culture fascinates sociologists nowadays, but this was not always the case. When I began teaching, in the early 1980s, material outcomes and structural explanations for social phenomena—such things as income, education, fertility changes, economic pressures—were under the sociological big top; culture and cultural explanations were a sideshow. True, there were always sociologists who studied religion, values, arts, and the like, and there were always anthropologists whose study of culture influenced sociological thinking. But as a whole, sociology did not pay much attention to culture.

As any teacher or student of sociology will know, times have changed. The past several years have witnessed an explosion of cultural studies in sociology, as well as in the adjacent social sciences of political science, psychology, and even economics. This rise of cultural studies has a number of causes, most generally the inherent limitations of strictly material factors to explain human behavior or to capture human experience. Therefore, most sociologists now view people as meaning makers as well as rational actors, symbol users as well as class representatives, and storytellers as well as points in a demographic trend. Moreover, sociology largely has escaped its former either/or way of thinking. The discipline now seeks to understand how people's meaning making shapes their rational action, how their class position molds their stories—in short, how social structure and culture mutually influence one another.

Although all of this is very satisfying to cultural sociologists who no longer have to think of themselves as laboring in the wilderness, problems bedevil teachers and students in the classroom. Everyone wants to talk about symbols, discourse, meaning, and cultural practices, but systematic guides to such discussions are rare. Needed are concise introductions to cultural sociology to help students (1) explore the concept of culture and the nature of its linkages with the social world, (2) enhance their understanding of seemingly structural issues such as poverty or ethnicity by applying cultural analysis to these issues, and (3) broaden their cultural and social horizons so that they may operate effectively in the global economy and international culture of the twenty-first century. These are the goals of this book.

The Cultural Diamond

Cultures and Societies in a Changing World will enable students taking broad-ranging courses in sociology or social problems and students taking specialized courses in cultural sociology to think more clearly about the role culture plays in shaping our social world. It introduces the sociology of culture, the branch of sociology that looks at cultural phenomena—including stories, beliefs, media, ideas, works of art, religious practices, fashions, rituals, specialized knowledge, and common sense—from a sociological perspective. At the same time, it suggests how such cultural phenomena operate in more general social processes. Finally, looking at the culture-society relationship from the other direction, it shows how social forces influence culture.

In the book, I use the device of the "cultural diamond" to investigate the connections among four elements: *cultural objects*—symbols, beliefs, values, and practices; *cultural creators*, including the organizations and systems that produce and distribute cultural objects; *cultural receivers*, the people who experience culture and specific cultural objects; and the *social world*, the context in which culture is created and experienced. We examine these elements and connections in Chapters 1 through 4. Then, in Chapters 5 and 6, we discuss how the cultural diamond operates in two specific cases: social problems and business transactions. In Chapter 7, we look at culture and community in the dawning age of global culture.

A Global Approach

An international or global outlook is indispensable to any sociological study in today's world, and cultural studies are no exception. This study of culture is global in at least three ways.

Cross-National Cases

First, we consider examples of cultural phenomena and processes from a wide variety of countries and periods. The world has always contained a bewildering assortment of cultures, of course, but lately Americans have become increasingly concerned with the implications of this fact for their internal social policies and external economic and political relationships. Although we examine aspects of the Western cultural tradition in general and American culture in particular, we also draw on materials from different traditions and cultures as well, including numerous examples from cultures of special interest to Americans, such as Israel and Japan.

Three countries—Nigeria, China, and the United States—serve repeatedly to demonstrate problems and issues in cultural analysis. These three countries constitute dramatically different starting points for societies entering the twenty-first century. Nigeria contains an extraordinary mixture of languages, ethnicities, and religions, with no one group in the majority. Under British colonial rule for more than half of the twentieth century, Nigeria struggles to reconcile political unity and cultural diversity while achieving greater economic development. China has had an advanced culture and centralized political control for millennia, but revolutionary political change in the mid-twentieth century has brought about massive social and cultural dislocations. Now China has embarked on an experiment with hitherto unheard of dimensions: to see whether economic freedom can flourish while tight political and cultural controls remain. The United States, along with its Western European allies, dominated the bipolar Cold War era of the mid-twentieth century. It seemed to represent the pinnacle of advanced, industrial society, complete with a modern culture, toward which all societies presumably were converging. Now the fracturing of former political alliances and the new complexity of international relations, along with the increasingly undeniable claims made by culturally diverse groups internally, challenge the validity of a specifically American culture and the applicability of American values in a troubled and rapidly changing world. For these reasons, Nigeria, China, and the United States offer thought-provoking running examples of some of the most perplexing culture problems facing the new century.

Global Culture

The second way in which this book is global in scope is that we consider how globalization processes themselves are affecting culture and cultures. From transnational media to tourist art to the immigration of peoples to international production of manufactured goods, processes taking place at the global level have all but obliterated pockets of cultural purity and have made parochialism increasingly costly as well as naive. Technological advances in communications have leaped cultural boundaries, just as global markets have transcended national differences; indeed, these two factors are closely related. The point is neither to celebrate nor bemoan these inexorable processes of globalization, but to understand them.

Cultural Conflicts

Third, many of the most intractable conflicts taking place in the post-Cold War era involve culture. Struggles over ethnic homogeneity and religious fundamentalism, to take just two examples particularly costly in human blood, clearly involve meanings and passions that go far beyond the mere economic or political. Similarly, negotiations between international business partners or heads of state, and more generally relations among people from different cultural backgrounds, can be smoother and more productive if the parties recognize the influences of different cultures. Understanding the cultural bases of past and current struggles and misunderstandings may help avoid repetition of costly mistakes. Such understanding will equip students to live their professional and personal lives as effective and wise citizens of a world where both cultures and societies are changing more quickly than ever before in human history.

Acknowledgments

In a book intended for teachers and students, it is appropriate to thank my own teachers and students. I developed my understanding of culture at Harvard University during the late 1970s under the guidance of a gifted group of teachers, including Orlando Patterson, Richard "Pete" Peterson, Paul Starr, Ann Swidler, and Harrison White; my studies were enlivened by conversations with fellow students pursuing some of the same objectives, including Mabel Berezin, Paul DiMaggio, and Jack Goldstone. I continue to benefit from scholarly communication and friendship with all of these people, as well as from the influence of colleagues I have met since, particularly including Howard Becker, Gary Fine, David Hummon, Elizabeth Long, Andrea Press, Robin Wagner-Pacifici, Bob Wuthnow, and Vera Zolberg.

Despite this valued circle of colleagues, however, perhaps the single most important influence on my thinking has been my students. For ten years I have both taught courses in the sociology of culture and have used a cultural emphasis in the introductory undergraduate course (Interaction, Community, and Culture), as well as the required graduate seminar at Chicago; I have also taught in Chicago's classic (50 years running) core course, Self, Culture, and Society. I have directed the Culture and Society Workshop for advanced graduate students, where some of our best and brightest pursue research involving the interaction between culture and society. In these courses and settings, students have asked the hard questions, come up with the apt examples, and challenged me to be clear in my thinking about how culture works and why it is important. My debt to these bright, infuriating, independent-minded, stubborn, and loyal students is immense. This book is for them.

Finally, I must thank my fellow editors of the Sociology for a New Century series, Charles Ragin and Larry Griffin, as well as Pine Forge Press founding editor Steve Rutter, who kept us all directed toward the common goal. One could not ask for a better team. Victoria Nelson applied her superb editing skills to my manuscript at both its shaping and polishing stages. My husband, colleague, and friend, John Padgett, provided intellectual and domestic support during the writing of this book, while Ray and Olivia provided distraction and delight.

1

Culture and the Cultural Diamond

Culture is one of those words that people use all the time but have trouble defining. Consider the following stories about some of the wildly different things we have in mind when we talk about culture.

> An American is doing business in Tokyo, hoping to land a lucrative contract for her firm. When her Japanese counterpart hands her his card, she takes it casually with one hand, glances at it, and sticks it in her pocket. Later, despite her best efforts, relations with her Japanese colleague remain chilly and her firm loses the contract. "Ah," says an experienced friend, "You lost the business because of a cultural misunderstanding. In Japan, the business card is considered to be an extension of the person; one treats the card with great respect, holding it with two hands and carefully putting it in a safe place. Americans don't think of it that way; for them, the card is just a convenience. You inadvertently insulted the very person you were trying to impress."

> It is Friday evening. In the dorm cafeteria, a group of college students are discussing their plans for the weekend. One says she is going to a basketball game, another says he plans to sleep all weekend, a third makes oblique references to a member of the opposite sex who is coming to visit. A fourth announces, "I'm going out to get some culture. I've got symphony tickets for tonight, and Sunday I'm meeting a friend at the art museum." His friends tease him about being a culture vulture, a label he stoutly rejects.

> Snorting with laughter, a husband reads aloud a "Calvin and Hobbes" comic strip to his wife at breakfast. In this episode, Calvin is telling Hobbes about a science fiction story in which machines turn human beings into "zombie slaves" (Watterson, 1988, p. 28). Hobbes agrees that the idea of machines controlling people is pretty scary, and Calvin replies, "I'll say. HEY! What time is it? My TV show is on!" The wife, who has been watching the *Today Show*, doesn't share his

amusement and coolly replies, "I hardly think reading comics is a more worthwhile cultural activity than watching television."

In an urban neighborhood where black and white residents come into contact daily, a sociologist named Elijah Anderson observes casual street encounters in which African Americans are visibly uncomfortable when they pass whites walking their dogs, despite the dog-walkers' assurances that their pets are friendly. This is the result of a cultural difference, he concludes (Anderson, 1990, p. 222):

> In the working-class black subculture, "dogs" does not mean "dogs in the house," but usually connotes dogs tied up outside, guarding the backyard, biting trespassers bent on trouble. Middle-class and white working-class people may keep dogs in their homes, allowing them the run of the house, but many black working-class people I interviewed failed to understand such behavior. When they see a white adult on his knees kissing a dog, the sight may turn their stomachs—one more piece of evidence attesting to the peculiarities of their white neighbors.

Recently bread—plain old bread—has taken on a certain élan. Bakers in upscale towns such as Berkeley have worked on improving the quality of American bread by introducing international baking techniques and new ingredients. And the trend is spreading. Boutique bakeries have become so successful that they have forced industry giants such as Pepperidge Farm to compete on their level. Americans raised on plain white bread now munch on Italian focaccia, seven-grain pita bread adapted from the Middle East, and sourdough baguettes that would amaze the French. New types of bread incorporating nine different stone-ground grains or hand-wrought into bread sticks receive fulsome tribute as being "first rate, handsomely crisp of crust and, yes, downright sexy" (Fabricant, 1992). Newspapers report this culinary development as a cultural shift.

Each of these five stories is about culture, but they all seem to be talking about very different things: national customs (handling business cards), activities considered to be elitist (e.g., attending the symphony), mass-produced forms of entertainment (comic strips), local variations in symbolic meanings (what dogs or bread represent). They also suggest that culture, though it may be something rather hard to pin down, is important to understand. Cultural ignorance or misunderstanding, it seems, can lead to highly undesirable outcomes: lost business, interracial tension, or an inability to participate in either the comic or the transcendent moments in human experience.

Cultural misunderstandings, cultural conflicts, cultural ignorance: The stakes can be very high. Consider a sixth story: Hindus revere a hilltop in Ayodhya, northern India, as the birthplace of the god Rama. But for centuries the Babri mosque, representing Islamic culture, has occupied this site. Despite India's political structure of secular democracy, tensions between Hindus and Muslims often run high. In 1992, they boiled over when fundamentalist Hindus, angry because they thought the government did not sufficiently support the dominant culture of the Hindus and convinced that Muslims were being coddled, tore down the mosque. Fighting erupted throughout India, and hundreds died.

What is this concept called culture that can apply to such a wide variety of situations? Why do notions of culture inflame such intense passions that huge numbers of people—from sectarians in Bombay to gang members flashing their signs in Chicago to nationalists in Northern Ireland—regularly kill for and die for their symbols, their beliefs, their cultures? And how can we gain a better understanding of the connections between the concept of culture and the social world? These are the questions addressed in this chapter.

Definitions: Two Ways of Looking at Culture

When sociologists talk about culture, Richard Peterson (1979) has observed, they usually mean one of four things: norms, values, beliefs, or expressive symbols. Roughly, norms are the way people behave in a given society, values are what they hold dear, beliefs are how they think the universe operates, and expressive symbols are representations, often representations of social norms, values, and beliefs themselves. We discuss later more about all four meanings, but for now the point is that even specialists such as sociologists and other academics use the word culture to stand for a whole range of ideas and objects.

The academic perspectives on culture can be sorted into two schools of thought. It is fair to say that most notions of culture are based on assumptions rooted either in the humanities on the one hand, or in the social sciences, particularly anthropology, on the other. Although this book presents the social scientific perspective by and large, the distinctiveness of this stance can be seen only in comparison with its counterpart in the humanities.

Before we begin, however, one thing needs to be clear: There is no such thing as "culture" or "society" out there in the real world. There are only people who work, joke, raise children, love, think, worship, and behave in a wide variety of ways. To speak of culture as one thing and society as another is to make an analytical distinction between two different aspects of human experience. One way to think of the distinction is that culture designates the expressive aspect of human existence, whereas society designates the relational (and often practical) aspect. Hugging dogs, paying respect to business cards, drawing comic strips—these are all ways in which we express our lives as social beings. The same object or behavior may be analyzed as social (a business card communicates information necessary for economic or personal transactions) or cultural (a business card means something different to a Japanese than to an American). Now, oriented with this rough distinction between the expressive versus the relational, and with a recognition that both culture and society are abstractions, we may explore the two most influential schools of thought about the culture/society relationship.

"The Best That Has Been Thought and Known"

In common usage, the term culture often refers to the fine and performing arts or to serious literature, as in the facetious statement of the symphony-goer, "I'm going out to get some culture." Culture in this sense is sometimes called "high culture"—as opposed to popular culture, folk culture, or mass culture—and it carries implications of high social status as well. The unthinking equation of culture with the arts is the result of a line of thinking, prominent in those disciplines collectively known as the humanities, whereby culture has been regarded as a locus of superior and universal worth.

In the nineteenth century, many European intellectuals posited an opposition between culture and society or, as they often put it, between culture and civilization. As they used the term, civilization referred to the technological advances of the Industrial Revolution so visible at that period and the social changes that attended industrialization. Contrasting culture with civilization was, therefore, a protest against Enlightenment thinking, against the belief that progress was invariably beneficial, against the ugly aspects of industrialization, and against what Marx called the "cash nexus" of capitalism whereby everyone and everything seemed to be evaluated on an economic basis. If "civilization" meant filthy tenements, factories spewing smoke into the air, and people treated as nothing more than so many replaceable parts, then many thoughtful men and women wanted no part of it. They saw culture—entailing the wisest and most beautiful expressions of human effort—as its contrasting pole and the salvation of overcivilized human beings. In this dichotomy, the alienating, dehumanizing effects of industrial civilization were set against the healing, life-enhancing capacities of culture. Typical of this polarizing tendency was the English social philosopher John Stuart Mill's account, in his auto-biography, of how his highly rationalized training in logic and economics brought him to a nervous breakdown. Only by reading Wordsworth's poetry, he testified, was he able to restore his sanity.

The automatic question that arises today occurred to nineteenth-century thinkers as well: How can we believe in culture's extraordinary, redeeming value without having this belief turn into a narrow ethnocentrism, a hymn of praise to Western European culture as the summit of human achievement? Matthew Arnold (1822-1888), a British educator and man of letters, answered this question by formulating a universal theory of cultural value ([1869] 1949). Emphasizing culture's potential influence in the social world, he harshly criticized Victorian England for its mindless materialism, for its worship of machines and freedom (in other words, industrialization and democracy) without considering the ends to which either should be put. He feared the result would be either dull, middle-class Philistinism[1] or social anarchy produced by rioting workers. There would be no help from the aristocrats, whom Arnold dismissed as "barbarians" too busy hunting foxes to bother about defending culture. Yet only culture could save modern society from such a fate.

What constituted this salvation of humankind? Culture, Arnold asserted, was "a study of perfection." Culture could make civilization more human by restoring "sweetness and light." Although it is now used pejoratively to convey superficial amiability, Arnold intended the expression "sweetness and light" to refer to beauty and wisdom, respectively. He took the idea of sweetness and light from Jonathan Swift's parable about the spiders versus the bees. Everyone thinks spiders are very industrious, Swift observed, but, in fact, spiders work only for themselves; all that web spinning is just to catch their own dinners. Bees, on the other hand, are more properly admirable, for they unselfishly produce benefits for others: honey and the wax used in making candles, or,

---

[1]As recounted in the Old Testament, the Philistines were one of the hostile tribes the Israelites encountered when they entered the promised land following their exile in Egypt and forty years in the wilderness. The Philistines were technologically more advanced than the Israelites in that they understood and employed metallurgy; the Israelites had to go to Philistine blacksmiths for metal tools and weapons. At the same time, the Israelites considered the Philistines to be culturally inferior because they worshipped a variety of deities. Thus the term Philistine refers to someone who may have practical knowledge and worldly success but who lacks spiritual and cultural refinement.

in other words, sweetness and light. Arnold appropriated the more socially productive of Swift's two creatures in his definition of culture. Like the honey and candles that come from bees, the beauty and wisdom that culture provides come from (1) awareness of and sensitivity to "the best that has been thought and known" in art, literature, history, and philosophy and (2) "a right reason" (an open-minded, flexible, tolerant intelligence).

How does culture work? Arnold, the educator, saw culture in terms of its educational potential. He maintained that culture enables people to relate knowledge, including science and technology, to conduct and to beauty. Civilization potentially has a harmonious relationship with knowledge, beauty, conduct, and social relations—this was a Greco-Roman view—and culture can bring about this harmony. Culture is not an end in itself, but a means to an end. It can cure the social ills of unrestrained materialism and self-satisfied Philistinism by teaching people how to live and by conveying moral ideas. In a sense, he believed, culture can be the humanizing agent that moderates the more destructive impacts of modernization.

Arnold's conception of culture holds that it addresses a different set of issues from those addressed by logic or science. Surprisingly, the German sociologist Max Weber (1864-1920), whom we shall encounter often in this book, took the same view. In his essay "Science as a Vocation," Weber laid out the limits of what science cannot do to set up his arguments about what science *can* do. The limits are what interest us here. What meaning for our lives can science offer? Weber suggested that it has none (1946, pp. 143, 153):

> Tolstoi has given the simplest answer, with the words: "Science is meaningless because it gives no answer to our question, the only question important for us: 'What shall we do and how shall we live?' " . . . Science today is a "vocation" organized in special disciplines in the service of self-clarification and knowledge of interrelated facts. It is not the gift of grace of seers and prophets dispensing sacred values and revelations, nor does it partake of the contemplation of sages and philosophers about the meaning of the universe.

To answer Tolstoi's question and find a meaning for their lives, Weber asserted, human beings must look to prophets and philosophers, to religion and ideas. Most generally, they must turn to culture.

Weber was a scientist and Arnold a man of letters, but both emphasized the separation of culture from everyday life in modern society and its ability to influence human behavior. This is the way of looking at culture traditionally associated with the humanities, although contemporary humanities disciplines are sharply questioning this approach. We can now summarize some of the general characteristics of this once-prevalent approach. The traditional humanities viewpoint:

- Evaluates some cultures and some cultural works as better than others; it believes culture has to do with perfection. Deriving from a root word meaning "cultivation," as in agriculture, this sense of culture entails the cultivation of the human mind and sensibility.

- Assumes that culture opposes the prevailing norms of the social order, or "civilization." A harmony between culture and society is possible, but rarely achieved.

- Fears that culture is fragile, that it can be "lost" or debilitated or estranged from socioeconomic life. Culture must be carefully preserved, through educational institutions, for example, and in cultural archives such as libraries and museums.

- Invests culture with the aura of the sacred and ineffable, thus removing it from everyday existence. This separation is often symbolically accentuated: The entrance to Chicago's main art museum (and many libraries and museums elsewhere), for example, is guarded by bronze lions. Because of its specialness, its extraordinary quality, culture makes no sense if we consider only its economic, political, or social dimensions.

"That Complex Whole"

During the nineteenth century, the new disciplines of anthropology and sociology were simultaneously advocating a very different way of thinking about culture than that put forth by Matthew Arnold. An early statement of this position came from the German philosopher Johann Gottfried Herder (1744-1803), who reacted strongly against the ethnocentric smugness of European culture at the end of the eighteenth century. Herder was fascinated by traditional folk verse and by the poetry of the Old Testament. He regarded such oral literature as spontaneous products of innate human creativity that sharply contrasted to the more artificial literary output of an educated elite. If all humanity were natural poets, how absurd to think that the European educated classes had somehow cornered the market on the "best that has been thought and known." Or as Herder put it,

> Men of all the quarters of the globe, who have perished over the ages, you have not lived solely to manure the earth with your ashes, so that at the end of time your posterity should be made happy by European culture. The very thought of a superior European culture is a blatant insult to the majesty of Nature. (quoted in Williams, 1976, p. 79)

Herder argued that we must speak of cultures, not simply culture, for the obvious reason that nations, and communities within or across nations, have their own, equally meritorious cultures. This view of culture as a given society's way of life was introduced to English anthropology by E. B. Tylor, who dismissed the whole culture-versus-civilization debate out of hand in his book *Primitive Culture* ([1871] 1958, p. 1): "Culture or Civilization, taken in its wide ethnographic sense, is that complex whole which includes knowledge, belief, art, morals, law, custom, and any other capabilities and habits acquired by man as a member of society." This wide-ranging anthropological definition of culture has dominated the social sciences, including contemporary sociology, ever since. The sociologist Peter Berger (1969), for example, defines culture as "the totality of man's products," both material and immaterial. Indeed, Berger argued that even society itself is "nothing but part and parcel of non-material culture" (pp. 6-7). Although social scientists don't all agree to quite so expansive a definition, they don't agree on much else about culture either. Back in the 1950s when two anthropologists counted the different definitions of culture used in the social sciences, they came up with more than 160 distinct meanings (Kroeber & Kluckhohn, 1952).

Viewing culture broadly as a people's entire way of life avoids the ethnocentrism and elitism that the humanities-based definition falls prey to, but such an all-encompassing definition lacks the precision desired in the social sciences. A recent trend has been toward cutting the culture concept down to size and making distinctions about exactly what the object of analysis is. Wuthnow and Witten (1988), for example, suggest that sociologists should distinguish between implicit and explicit culture. Sometimes we regard culture as a tangible social construction, "a kind of symbolic good or commodity that is explicitly produced" (p. 50), as in the case of a Calvin and Hobbes cartoon, a loaf of bread, or a symphony. At other times, culture is seen more abstractly as an "implicit feature of social life ... a prefiguration or ground of social relations" (p. 50), as in the cultural ground whereby Japanese and Americans handle business cards in different ways or American blacks and whites act differently around dogs. This distinction is useful, not because either kind of culture is conceptually superior, but because it can act as a preliminary classification in sorting out all of the many definitions of culture with which sociologists must deal.

Unlike the old-school humanists, social scientists of various schools of thought tend to see harmony, not opposition, between culture and society. The two most influential social scientific theories of the twentieth century regard the fit as being a close one. Functionalism, the branch of social theory that assumes a social institution usually serves some specific function necessary for the well-being of the collectivity, identifies culture with the values that direct the social, political, and economic levels of a social system. In the functionalist perspective, it follows, a fit exists between culture and society because any misfit would be dysfunctional. The functionalist sociologist Robert Merton (1938), for example, once suggested that American culture places a high value on economic success. When people lack the practical means to attain the goal of success, he said, they experience severe strain, often turning to criminal behavior as a result. For most people in America and in any culture that functions smoothly, the goals given by the culture and the means for attaining these goals work in harmony. Coming from the opposite direction politically, Marxists also see a close fit between social structure and culture, but they reverse the direction of influence—from social structure to culture, not the other way around. Both functionalism and Marxism are discussed in Chapter 2; the point for now is that they share what we might call the "close fit assumption."

As an example of this assumption, consider Peter Berger's (1969) analysis of culture as formed through externalization, objectification, and internalization. Berger suggests that human beings project their own experience onto the outside world (externalization), then regard these projections as independent (objectification), and finally incorporate these projections into their psychological consciousness (internalization). We can easily think of cases that seem to illustrate Berger's model. Let's take the fact that human reproduction involves two sexes. Many religious belief systems might be said to externalize the dualism of biological reproduction into dual powers, such as the Manichean worldview of an eternal war between good and evil or the Chinese dualities of yin and yang. Such dualities, based on direct experience, become objectified and exist in the culture independent of any human thinker. Entire cosmologies of contending forces of good and evil are thereby built around the male-female dichotomy. These cosmologies, in turn, become internalized, influencing human thought and practice. Thus Christians have the image of good and evil fighting within the soul—an angel whispering in one ear, a devil in the other— while Chinese medicine is developed around the perceived need for a yin and yang balance in the body itself.

Anthropologist Clifford Geertz (1973, p. 89) defined culture as "an historically transmitted pattern of meanings embodied in symbols, a system of inherited conceptions expressed in symbolic forms by means of which men communicate, perpetuate, and develop their knowledge about and attitudes toward life." Geertz's influential formulation is more precise than the entire-way-of-life social science definitions because it focuses on symbols and on the behavior that derives from symbolically expressed ways of thinking and feeling. This definition captures what most sociologists currently mean when they use the term culture. To recapitulate, the social science standpoint:

- Avoids evaluation in favor of relativism. As two sociologists put it, "The scientific rhetoric, tight-lipped and non-normative, brooks no invidious distinctions" (Jaeger & Selznick, 1964, p. 654). Evaluations may be made in terms of the impact that culture has on the social order, but not of the cultural phenomenon itself.

- Assumes a close linkage between culture and society. In some schools of thought, one tends to determine the other, whereas others stress the mutual adjustments that take place between culture and social structure.

- Emphasizes the persistence, the durability of culture, rather than its fragility. Culture is seen more as an activity than as something that needs to be preserved in an archive. Culture is not what lies in the museum or library guarded by those bronze lions; instead, it is the ways in which museum-goers (and everyone else) live their lives.

- Assumes that culture can be studied empirically like anything else. Social scientists do not regard culture as sacred or as fundamentally different from other human products and activities.

One might well respond to the distinction we have been setting between the traditional humanities and the social scientific approaches by saying, "Look, there are advantages to both points of view. To understand why Indian Hindus and Muslims are willing to die for their cultures, it helps to see that their adherents regard their religious beliefs as very special, 'the best that has been thought and known,' and thus extraordinarily valuable. At the same time, an understanding of the political and economic contexts—the links between religion on the one hand and Indian social structure on the other—is obviously necessary to comprehend and explain the recurring explosions of sectarian violence. So why not try to understand culture by approaching it from both directions?"

Why not, indeed? In this book, although our object is a specifically sociological understanding of culture, we try to incorporate the insights of both traditions. We begin to do so by envisioning the culture/society connection in terms of "cultural objects" located in a "cultural diamond."

Connections: The Links Between Culture and Society

We have been looking at various definitions of culture, from the most restrictive (high art; "the best that has been thought and known") to the most expansive (the totality of humanity's material and nonmaterial products). We have seen that the word and the concept, especially as employed in the social sciences, takes many shapes and that therefore any discussion of culture must begin with a definition. Here, then, is our working definition: Culture refers to the expressive side of human life—behavior, objects, and ideas that can be seen to express, to stand for, something else. This is the case whether we are talking about explicit or implicit culture.

Geertz, and Weber before him, took culture to involve meaning, and in this book we follow their example. Thus, we could talk about a community in terms of its culture: its pattern of meanings, its enduring expressive aspects, its symbols that represent and guide the thinking, feeling, and behavior of its members. Or we could talk about that community in terms of social structure: its pattern of relationships among members, its institutions, its economic and political factors. The community's culture influences its social structure, and vice versa; indeed, the two are intertwined and have been separated only for purposes of analysis. To understand the community, the sociologist must understand both.

We need to do more, however, than simply define culture and indicate how to distinguish it analytically from social structure. We need a way to conceptualize how culture and the social world come together or, in other words, how people in social contexts create meaning. To draw on both the humanities and social science views for our analysis of culture and to examine cultural phenomena and their relation to social life, we need a conceptual framework and conceptual tools. One of these tools is the cultural object.

The Cultural Object

A cultural object may be defined as shared significance embodied in form (Griswold, 1986). In other words, it is a socially meaningful expression that is audible, or visible, or tangible, or can be articulated. A cultural object, moreover, tells a story, and that story may be sung, told, set in stone, enacted, or painted on the body. Examples range widely. A Nigerian proverb such as "A toad does not run at noonday for nothing,"[2] a religious

---

[2]This is an Igbo proverb from Eastern Nigeria. Its meaning is roughly equivalent to our saying "Where there's smoke, there's fire."

doctrine such as the Trinity, a belief that women are more sensitive than men, a Shakespearean sonnet, a hairstyle such as Rastafarian dreadlocks or the Manchu queue, a habit of saying "God bless you" when somebody sneezes, a quilt made by hand or by robots—any and all of these can be cultural objects. Each tells a story. Notice that the status of cultural object is the result of an analytic decision that we make as observers; it is not something built into the object itself. If we think of the quilt as a product in a department store's inventory or something to warm our feet in bed, and not in terms of its meaning, the quilt is not a cultural object. But when it is considered in terms of its story—how it expresses women collectively piecing together scraps to produce an object of beauty and utility—then the quilt becomes a meaningful cultural object and may be analyzed as such.

In this book, we talk equally of "cultural objects" and "culture," so it is important to keep the terms straight. Specifying a cultural object is a way of grasping some part of the broader system we refer to as culture and holding up that part for analysis. One might compare this distinction to how we would go about studying a marsh. We would need to analyze the soil, the water, the climate, and the specific forms of animal and plant life found there (e.g., the leopard frog) in order to understand how the ecosystem works as a whole. On the other hand, if we were primarily interested in a particular species of frog, our study would concentrate on it, with the marsh as biological context. Analogizing to our terms, the cultural object is the leopard frog, and the culture is the marsh.

In attempting to understand the connections between a society and its culture, it seems to make sense to start the analysis with a close examination of cultural objects, those smaller parts of the interrelated larger system. Here we are following the lead of the humanities: Culture *is* in a world apart, at least for analytical purposes. Literary critics, art historians, and others in the humanities usually focus on a work of art as a self-referential universe possessing structure and meaning. This practice seems sound for examining cultural objects in our wider social sciences definition. We start, therefore, by paying close attention to the cultural object itself. This does not imply an "art for art's sake" (or culture for culture's sake) rejection of the external world and how it impinges on the cultural object, but simply means we first take the cultural object as evidence about itself. In other words, we start with the cultural object, though we certainly don't end there.

Let's go back to bread, the homely subject of our fifth story, and think of it now as a cultural object. Americans and Europeans eat a lot of bread, but they don't pay a great deal of attention to it. Bread is basic, fundamental, at the foundation of the nutrition pyramid (yawn). Bread is practical. Bread is also very boring.

Practical and boring though it may be, bread can be expressive as well. The post-World War II baby boom generation, for example, grew up on soft, spongy white bread like Wonder Bread. The "wonder" lay in the technology—Wonder bread was infused with vitamins to "grow strong bodies in 12 ways"—and although it didn't have an especially memorable flavor, baby boomers who spread it with concoctions such as peanut butter and marshmallow fluff thought it tasted just fine. It seemed to express a child's view of the good life. Later, in the 1960s and 1970s, that same baby boom generation rejected white bread, just as it rejected much else from mainstream American culture; defying the conventions they had grown up with, these young people turned eating whole-grain bread into a political statement, one that expressed a repudiation of American capitalism, technology, and homogeneity.

Not only can bread be expressive, but a moment's reflection reminds us that it is steeped in tradition. The Bible abounds in references to bread: It is the staff of life, it is unleavened during Passover, it is miraculously multiplied along with the fishes, it should be cast upon the waters. In the Christian communion, it even embodies the Divine. During the first centuries of Islam, white bread symbolized a lack of discipline to the Arabs; a manuscript illustration shows a man enjoying a self-indulgent meal of roast kid, wine, and white bread (Tannahill, 1973, p. 173). In the European ethnic heritage that has shaped many American institutions, bread connotes security, love, frugality, family, even life itself.

We further recognize that although bread may be ubiquitous in American kitchens, it is by no means universal. Human beings eat different grains in different places: Many Chinese depend on rice, Senegalese on millet, Mexicans on corn. In some of these countries, eating bread is a sign of being Westernized, being modern, and it can become a political issue. In Nigeria, which enjoyed a period of oil-based wealth during the 1970s, the middle class developed a taste for bread made from imported flour and a distaste for local starches such as yam and cassava. White bread connotes affluence and modernity for twentieth-century Nigerians just as it did for eighteenth-century Europeans. In the poorer "oil-bust" years beginning in the 1980s, however, taxes on imports plus government advocacy of using locally produced foods attempted to shift Nigerian consumer tastes back to West African traditional starches. The battle has not been altogether successful, however, and the streets of Lagos are filled with young hawkers of high-priced spongy white bread, something like our old friend Wonder bread.

So bread is basic, fundamental, and boring—but it is also biblically sanctioned, expressive, symbolic of European heritage or the good life, and even sexy. It is as much a part of a cultural system—whether we think of the local cultural system (the latest gustatory trends in Berkeley) or the global cultural system (the meaning of white bread in Nigeria)—as the more obviously "cultural" artifacts such as television or ballet. Bread, then, is clearly a cultural object. Cultural objects are part of a larger cultural system that we may want to analyze. How do the myriad components in this system mesh together? To look at the bigger picture of culture in society, we need another analytical tool.

The Cultural Diamond

Cultural objects are made by human beings. This fact is intrinsic to all of the various definitions—culture is "the best that has been thought and known" *by human beings* (Arnold); culture is the "meanings embodied in symbols" *through which human beings* communicate and pass on knowledge and attitudes (Geertz); culture is the externalization, objectification, and internalization *of human experience* (Berger)—and is the basis for the familiar distinction between culture and nature. Therefore, we may regard all cultural objects as having creators. These creators may be the people who first articulate and communicate an idea, the artists who fashion a form, the inventors of a new game or new lingo. Any particular object may have a single creator, such as the author of a novel, or multiple creators, such as all of the people listed in the credits at the beginning of a movie.

Other people besides their creators experience cultural objects, of course. If a poet sings her odes in the wilderness with no one to hear or record, if a hermit invents a revolutionary new theology but keeps it to himself, if a radio program is broadcast but a technical malfunction prevents anyone from hearing it, then these are potential cultural objects but not actual ones. It is only when such objects become public, when they enter the circuit of human discourse, that they enter the culture and become cultural objects. Therefore, all cultural objects must have people who receive them, people who hear, read, understand, think about, enact, participate in, remember them. We might call these people the object's audience, although that term is a bit misleading; the people who actually experience the object may be different from the intended or original audience, and far from being a passive audience, cultural receivers are active meaning makers.

Both cultural objects and the people who create and receive them are not floating freely, but are anchored in a particular context. We can call

Figure 1-1

The Cultural Diamond

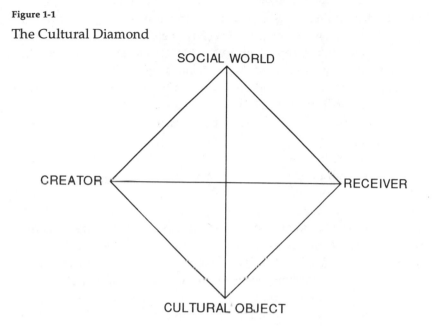

this the social world, by which we mean the economic, political, social, and cultural patterns and exigencies that occur at any particular point in time. Cultural sociology is concerned, first and foremost, with the relationship between cultural objects and the social world.

We have identified four elements: creators, cultural objects, recipients, and the social world. Let us first arrange these four elements in the shape of a diamond and then draw a line connecting each element to every other one. Doing this creates what I call a cultural diamond (a diamond in the two-dimensional sense of a baseball diamond), which looks like Figure 1-1.

Our cultural diamond has four points and six links or connections. We cannot call it a theory of culture because it says nothing about how the points are related. Nor can we call it a model of culture in the strict sense, because it does not indicate cause and effect; in the cultural diamond, violence in the popular culture (e.g., television programs) could be seen as "causing" violence in the social world, but the reverse could equally be the case. Instead, the cultural diamond is an accounting device intended to encourage a fuller understanding of any cultural object's relationship to the social world. It does not say what the relationship between any of the points should be, only that there *is* a relationship.

Therefore, a complete understanding of a given cultural object would require understanding all four points and six links. To understand bread in Berkeley and in Lagos, we would have to know about the producers (the growers, bakers, importers, trend-setting chefs and restaurant owners, government bureaucrats setting import controls) and the consumers (the population and its demographic characteristics—how many children are packing lunches, how many working couples are eating out, how an aging and increasingly thrifty population is gratifying its tastes for luxury, how the public has come to associate white bread with prosperity). We would need to understand linkages—the media connections advertising products to consumers, for example, or the system of distribution whereby teenage boys acquire fresh bread to hawk on the highways. Only when such points and connections had been investigated could we be confident that we understood the relationship—a specifically cultural relationship— that exists between bread and the society in which it is made and eaten.

The same is true for any aspect of culture that we isolate and analyze as a cultural object: We need to identify the characteristics of the object and how it is like some other objects in the culture and unlike others. We need to consider who created (made, formed, said) it and who received (heard, saw, believed) it. We need to think about the various linkages; for example, on the social world/creator link, how is it that in this society some types of people get to be the creators of this type of cultural object and others do not? (For example, think about how women have often been excluded from creating certain kinds of cultural objects.) On the cultural object/audience link, how is it that some cultural objects reach an audience and others do not? (For example, think about all of the poems that never get published or all of the plays that never get produced.) Once we understand the specific points and links in the diamond, we can say that we have a sociological understanding of that cultural object. Moreover, once we have a sense of how that cultural object fits into its context, we are on our way to understanding the culture as a whole.

Summary

In this chapter, we have seen the variety of ways in which the term culture is used and how the term is applied to ephemeral, even trivial, aspects of experience and to deeply held values for which people are willing to die. We have compared the humanities' approach to culture with that of the social sciences and have suggested that a full understanding of the relationship between culture and society must employ the insights of both perspectives. We have suggested an approach to the sociological analysis of culture that uses the conceptual tools of cultural object and cultural diamond as a schema for organizing our thinking and investigation.

In the following chapters, we apply the cultural diamond schema to the complex web of connections between cultures and societies. The chapters are organized following the diamond: In Chapter 2, we concentrate on the meanings found in cultural objects (the social world/cultural object link); in Chapter 3, we examine creators of cultural objects (the diamond's left point); and in Chapter 4, we focus on systems of production (the links between creators, receivers, and cultural objects) and receivers or audiences themselves (the right point). In Chapters 5 and 6, we turn to two applications of sociologically informed cultural analysis: social problems and organizational transactions. In Chapter 7, we consider the relationship of culture and community in the global, postmodern social world of the new century.

RECOMMENDED FOR FURTHER READING

Anderson, Elijah. 1990. *Streetwise: Race, Class, and Change in an Urban Community.* Chicago: University of Chicago Press. A sociologist working in Philadelphia and an African American intent on understanding the lives of people in the inner city, Anderson has written a masterly account of the interaction of culture and social structure in today's urban America.

Geertz, Clifford. 1973. *The Interpretation of Cultures.* New York: Basic Books. This collection of essays by a cultural anthropologist is probably the most influential book on culture in decades. In a variety of cultural settings, including especially North Africa and Java, Geertz exemplifies the Weberian injunction for social scientists to study meaning.

Williams, Raymond. 1976. *Keywords: A Vocabulary of Culture and Society.* New York: Oxford University Press. A Marxian literary critic, Williams gives the history of a number of terms that are important in the social sciences, including culture, and shows how such terms are by no means innocent of class-based assumptions.

2

Cultural Meaning

They said, "You have a blue guitar,
You do not play things as they are."
The man replied, "Things as they are
Are changed upon the blue guitar."
And they said then, "But play, you must,
A tune beyond us, yet ourselves,
A tune upon the blue guitar
Of things exactly as they are."

(Stevens, [1936] 1954, p. 165)

Wallace Stevens, a Connecticut insurance executive who also happened to be one of the most important American poets of the twentieth century, wrote "The Man With the Blue Guitar" as a commentary on the ambiguous relationship between poetry and what most people regard as the "real world." What he said about poetry applies more generally to culture and to cultural objects. We sense that culture is "beyond us, yet ourselves," and we look for a simple relationship between cultural objects and "things exactly as they are." But there is no simple relationship, for when something becomes a cultural object—when, as it were, it is played upon the blue guitar—that something is indeed changed. And the change involves meaning.

By definition, a cultural object has shared significance—it has been given a meaning shared by members of the culture. In the aggregate, as Geertz's definition in Chapter 1 emphasizes, a culture is a "pattern of meanings" passed down over time. Meaning or significance (we use the two terms interchangeably) refers to the object's capacity—in addition to whatever practical or direct properties it may have—to suggest or point to something else. Thus the sound of a fire alarm "means" that everyone should clear the building, or an A on a test "means" that the student has mastered the material. Each of the stories that opened Chapter 1 is a parable about meaning. In the first story, for example, the Japanese businessman attached personal significance to his business card, whereas the same card had no meaning to the American beyond its practical function. Because they misunderstood each other's cultural structure, a business deal was lost. In the fourth story, dogs were significant cultural objects to both middle-class whites and working-class blacks in the neighborhood Anderson studied, but they meant different things to each group. Anderson, the analyst, found that these different meanings were themselves meaningful as cultural indicators of social phenomena.

We can identify two types of meaning: simple and complex. Simple meaning denotes one-to-one correspondence. We express this type of meaning when we talk about signs and what they stand for. Algebra uses signs in this manner; in the equation $a^2 + b^2 = c^2$ we know that a "means" the length of one leg of a right triangle, b "means" the length of the other leg, and c "means" the length of the hypotenuse. Likewise, a flashing red light "means" stop, then go. All of these signs have a single referent.

Complex meaning is found in the signs typically called symbols. Rather than standing for a single referent, symbols evoke a variety of meanings, some of which may be ambiguous. Symbols do not denote; they connote, suggest, imply. They evoke powerful emotions—think how many people have died for a flag—and can often both unite and disrupt social groups. A few years ago, for example, a Christian student association erected a giant cross at the University of Ibadan, the most prestigious university in Nigeria. Now the cross is a symbol that draws up a variety of deep-seated images, attitudes, and beliefs in Christians. This cross, however, happened to cast a long shadow over the Islamic student mosque in the afternoon sun. To the Muslim students, this accident of position symbolized the (literal) overshadowing of Islam by Christianity—an implied meaning they vehemently rejected. They retaliated by building a wall symbolizing their Islamic religious pride that blocked the shadow.

Because it is complex, culture is made up of complex rather than simple meanings—meanings "embodied in symbols," to continue with Geertz's definition. To understand culture, we need to be able to unravel these tangled webs of meanings. In other words, we need to be able to analyze the relationship that may exist between a symbol, the "tune upon the blue guitar," on the one hand, and "things exactly as they are" on the other. This relationship, of course, can be highly personal and individual, as when a psychoanalyst analyzes a patient's dreams for their symbolic content. The sociology of culture, however, looks for social meanings. And in our cultural diamond, what links cultural objects with the social worlds is meaning.

In this chapter, we consider why the need for meaning is fundamental to human existence. We then consider an influential theoretical model that suggests that cultural meaning comes from culture's capacity to mirror social life. We investigate the classical roots of this "reflection" model and two contemporary sociological versions of it: functionalist and Marxist cultural theories. Then we look at Max Weber's striking reversal of the mirror model in his assertion that the social world actually reflects culture, not the other way around. Finally, we look at some contemporary sociological applications of reflection theory.

Why Do We Need Meaning?

We all know that living beings grow and act according to instructions encoded in their genes. In animals, we call this genetic prompting of behavior instinct; for example, a hare instinctively knows to run from the scent of a fox but not the scent of a chipmunk. Most of what animals do and know is genetically given—hardwired, so to speak. Human beings are different. In the first place, they are physiologically incomplete when they are born. The large size of the human head requires that a baby be born before all of its internal systems are finished; it has been said that human "life" independent of the mother doesn't really begin until the child is several months old. More to the point, human genetic encodings do not provide sufficient information for survival. A kitten, once weaned, could survive in the woods without other members of its species to show it what to do, but a 1-year-old child could not. Humans must learn to live. And learning in humans is a social process of interaction and socialization whereby culture is transmitted.

Anthropologists have stressed how the total of such human interactions transmits patterns of meanings and behaviors and that these patterns are called culture. Consider Geertz's (1973, pp. 45-46) summary of how human culture compensates for genetic incompleteness:

> Man is so in need of . . . symbolic sources of illumination to find his bearings in the world because the nonsymbolic sort that are constitutionally ingrained in his body cast so diffused a light. The behavior patterns of lower animals are, at least to a much greater extent, given to them with their physical structure; genetic sources of information order their actions within much narrower ranges of variation, the narrower and more thoroughgoing the lower the animal. For man, what are innately given are extremely general response capacities. . . . Undirected by culture patterns—organized systems of significant symbols—man's behavior would be virtually ungovernable, a

mere chaos of pointless acts and exploding emotions, his experience virtually shapeless. Culture, the accumulated totality of such patterns, is not
just an ornament of human existence but . . . an essential condition for it.

Peter Berger (1969) suggested, along similar lines, that the ultimate human
terror is not evil, but chaos. A total absence of order, a world without
structure or meaning, is so horrifying as to be unthinkable. As a bulwark
against chaos, human beings create cultures through the externalization/
objectification/internalization process we examined earlier, thereby constructing the worlds in which they operate.

Thus, the sociological analysis of culture begins at the premise that
culture provides orientation, wards off chaos, and directs behavior toward certain lines of action and away from others. Culture provides
meaning and order through the use of symbols, whereby certain things
that we have designated as cultural objects are endowed with signifi
cance over and above their material utility. We can most easily see this in
the case of tangible or visible objects—business cards, dogs, works of art—
but the same is true for ideas or bits of behavior as well. The attributes of
a desirable husband, for example, or the social script in which a young
woman looks at a man, lowers her eyes for a moment, and then looks at
him again are cultural objects that carry meaning. In some cultures, rural
Italy perhaps, the aforementioned young woman's behavior would be
appropriate; in others, it would be a coy, irritating display of pseudoin-
nocence; in still others, it would be considered as immodest and even
whorish. Likewise, in West African cultures, such as that of the Yoruba,
patterned facial scars mean that a man has kinship affiliations that make
him either desirable or off-limits as a suitor. In other societies, these scars
would be considered as either irrelevant or disfiguring. Neither scars nor
lowering the eyes has meaning in and of itself, but both become intensely
meaningful insofar as they are embedded in a culture that produces or
interprets them.

Culture and Meaning in Reflection Theory

If culture involves meanings, and if meanings are social, then again we
must ask: What types of relationships exist between the social world and
cultural objects or patterns? The basic questions are, Where does meaning
come from? and What difference do meanings make? Two of the most
important sociological answers to this question—those provided by functionalism and Marxism—we can consider as versions of reflection theory,

whereby culture is seen as a faithful reflection of social life. The third answer, that offered by Max Weber, emphasizes the degree to which social life reflects culture. We need to take a careful look at the whole idea of reflection and the implications of this model for how we think about culture. We start by considering the background of the reflection model in classical Greek thought. Equipped with this background, we explore the forms that reflection theory has taken in functionalism, Marxism, and Weberian analysis.

Culture as Mirror

The assumption behind the idea of culture as reflection is a simple one: Culture is the mirror of social reality. Therefore, the meaning of a particular cultural object lies in the social structures and social patterns it reflects. The sociologically informed analyst, it follows, should look for direct, one-to-one correspondences between culture and society.

The reflection model has much to recommend it, including common sense. Most people believe, for example, that the violence and mayhem depicted on television reflect the violence and mayhem in our society. This is not to deny that television violence may itself contribute to social violence. These are simply two different connections on the cultural diamond that may or may not vary together but that are conceptually distinct, as indicated in Figure 2-1. In one conceptualization, television violence is a reflection of the social world; in the other, the social world is a reflection of television violence. Traditionally, cultural sociology has preferred the former way of describing the connection, asking how it is that culture reflects society and admitting the latter way—how society reflects culture — only as a secondary consideration.

Putting this simple reflection model on our cultural diamond, as in Figure 2-1, shows how we might go about testing common beliefs about the connection between television and violence. If the question is, Does television reflect changes in the social world? we would measure incidents of violence in a given society at some starting point (T1) until some later point (T2). We similarly would measure changes in violent episodes on television over the same time. Our expectation, following reflection theory, would be that television violence, allowing for a certain time lag, would rise and fall along with the rates of real-life violence. That does not mean that social violence *causes* television violence, only that there is a correlation between the two. If, on the other hand, the two rates rise and fall together but the ups and downs in television violence *precede*

Figure 2-1

Reflection Model of Television and Violence

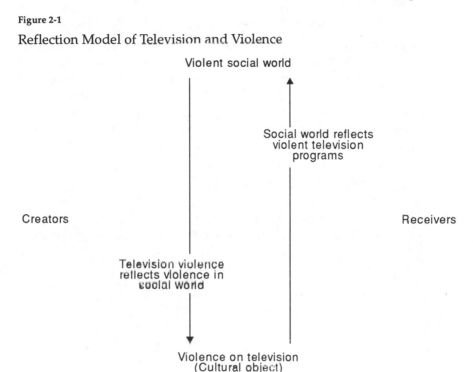

corresponding changes in the rate of social violence, this would support the social-world-reflects-culture argument.

Besides, according with our common-sense observations of the way the world works, reflection theory gains credibility from the fact that artists, writers, and other cultural creators often describe what they do in these terms. As the nineteenth-century French writer Stendhal responded to critics who accused him of portraying sordid materials ([1830] 1958, p. 363),

> A novel, gentlemen, is a mirror carried along a highway. Sometimes it re-
> flects to your view the azure of the sky, sometimes the mire of the puddles
> in the road. And the man who carries the mirror on his back will be accused
> by you of immorality! His mirror shows the mire and you blame the mirror!

As well as having both a great deal of plausibility and the endorsement of modern culture creators, reflection theories of culture also have a long history. Like so much else, they go back to Plato. A brief review of the history of the reflection model will show how certain assumptions about the relationship between culture and the "real world" have entered into sociological models.

The Greek Background to Reflection Theory

We begin our consideration of the classical origins of reflection theory with Plato (c. 430-347 B.C.), Athenian philosopher and student of Socrates. According to Plato's theory of forms, advanced in book 10 of *The Republic*, behind all appearances lies an idea or a form. For example, although we sleep on a physical bed, the physical piece of furniture is mere appearance. Reality is a preexisting form, Bed. The physical bed reflects this ideal bed, but it does so imperfectly. Human beings, however, confuse appearance for reality, just as when people in a cave take as reality the flickering shadows a fire throws on the wall.

Even appearances come from somewhere, and Plato suggested that they come from reflection. He asked, How could someone—a cultural creator, we would say—make all of the works of the universe, all of nature, all of the heavens, all of the gods? Impossible, said a student, but Plato replied:

> There are many ways in which the feat might be quickly and easily accomplished, none quicker than that of turning a *mirror* round and round—you would soon enough make the sun and the heavens, and the earth and yourself, and other animals and plants, and all the other things of which we were just now speaking, in the mirror.

Plato thus envisioned three types of creators: (1) God, the creative being, who makes the one real bed in its ideal form, (2) the carpenter who makes a physical bed, and (3) the painter who makes a picture of the physical bed. Thus art, such as that produced by the painter, is an imperfect copy of an imperfect copy and is based on a low, irrational understanding of what beds (or anything else) are all about. All art—hence all mimesis or imitation—is a long way from truth; the artist can imitate so many things because he or she has only a superficial understanding of any of them. In Plato's view, human life is a pilgrimage from appearance to reality. Art presents an obstacle to this journey because it seduces people into a false or brute understanding of life, whereby they think they see what is real.

Note some features of this argument: Plato links his objection to art based on the theory of forms with his objection based on the educational function of culture. Of course, the two need not go together. As we have seen, Matthew Arnold made the liberal argument that art, like all culture, widens experience, thus making people more sensitive and selective. Notice as well the religious basis of Plato's objections. Good art does not imitate divine patterns, it participates in them. This view is comparable to the Islamic view of art, which forbids representation of living things; according to Islamic aesthetic theory, art involves good designs but should not compete with Allah's creation. Such religious objections to the representation of living things are common, as witness the Judeo-Christian second commandment: "You shall not make for yourself a graven image, or any likeness of anything that is in heaven above, or that is in the earth beneath, or that is in the water under the earth" (Exodus 21:4 [RSV]).

Thus, Plato's theory of forms has three components: the form, the appearance, and the art. Translating into our terminology, we could say there are the idea, the material embodiment of the idea, and the symbolic or cultural expression of the idea, thus forming a double-diamond, as in Figure 2 2. But the consequence of this three-part structure was, for Plato, a downgrading of the third term as being doubly removed from reality.

Aristotle (384-322 B.C.), a younger contemporary of Plato and a member of his academy, suggested a way to defend art (and, by extension, culture): Redefine the middle term. He argued that art imitates not the ideal realm, but universal truths about human existence. Aristotle's redefinition—art imitates the universals of nature—was to change the very meaning of mimesis. Aristotle's universalism is the basis for Matthew Arnold's "best that has been thought and known" (and indeed for much of humanist thinking), for one of the distinguishing characteristics of "the best" is its broad range of applicability.

Reflection theory in its Platonic origins implies that culture is less than real, less fundamental than what it reflects, and this implication has carried over into the discipline of sociology. So have the more positive Aristotelian twists of this theory—that culture is somehow more profound than the social world and that culture can represent human universals. The two dominant sociological theories of the twentieth century—functionalism and Marxism—both employ the reflection model, and both perpetuate some of its Platonic implications. Both also exhibit the "close-fit assumption" between culture and society that earlier was described as characteristic of social science theories of culture in general. Now we see where this idea comes from: If one entity "reflects" another, then it has to match that other entity very closely. Let us examine the cultural implications of these two sociological theories, seeking both the strengths and the deficiencies of their versions of the reflection model.

Culture and Meaning in Marxian Sociology

Like all social theorists, Karl Marx and his collaborator Frederick Engels were responding to the intellectual and social currents of their own day, the mid-nineteenth century. In their early writings about culture—and

Figure 2-2

Plato's Reflection Theory Set on the Cultural Diamond

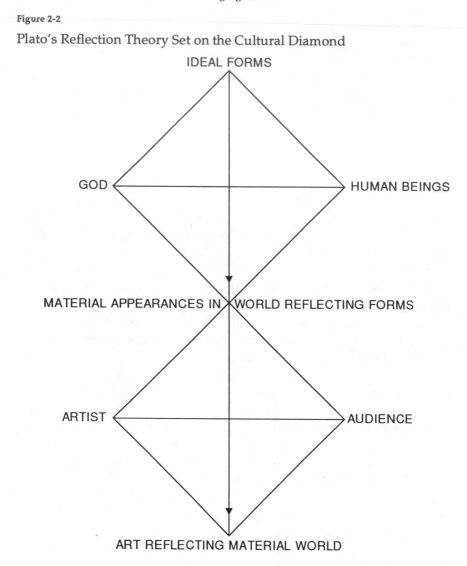

Marx's cultural analysis was produced mostly in the early part of his career, before he turned his attention more exclusively to economics— Marx and Engels were engaged in the philosophical debate between idealism and materialism. We have already been introduced to idealism in the Platonic version. Now we take a look at the debate as it appeared some 2,000 years after Plato, when Marx was a young man.

"From Earth to Heaven":
The Materialist Approach to Culture

As we have seen, the basic premise of idealism is that culture can best be understood as the embodiment of ideas, spirit, beauty, and universal truth. As such, it is separate and autonomous from material or earthly existence. The late-eighteenth and early-nineteenth-century thinkers known as the German Idealists shared the neo-Platonic sense that the spirit, the idea, the intellectual category was antecedent to sensuous empirical reality. Immanuel Kant (1724-1804), for example, argued that the human mind could only receive and respond to the external world because the mind possessed concepts such as time and space before experiencing them empirically. G. W. F. Hegel (1770-1831) made idealism into a principle of world history. Hegel postulated a World Spirit that moved toward fulfillment at the end of history. Every age, he said, had a unitary character because its culture, politics, and historical events all manifested the World Spirit at a given stage of development. Why do things change? Hegel maintained that history moves through conflicts between irreconcilable forces. During some periods, one force dominates (the thesis), but its domination breeds new crises (the antithesis), and eventually the dominant ideas and forces are overthrown and replaced by a new force that reconciles the old thesis and antithesis (the synthesis). This synthesis becomes the new thesis, it breeds conflicts, and so on; history moves on through stages in a series of revolutions.

If idealism gives the ideal precedence over the material, materialism reverses the relationship. Karl Marx (1818-1883) encountered materialist thought in 1836, when, at the age of eighteen, he came to the University of Berlin (from which he received a doctorate in post-Aristotelian Greek philosophy in 1841) and became involved with the Young Hegelians. The Young Hegelians were a group concerned with turning Hegelian philosophy to more progressive ends. Critical social thinkers, they wanted to expose laws of history in order to reform society; thus, they were "idealists" in the everyday sense of the term, as well as in the philosophical sense.

After finishing his degree and realizing that a university career would be impossible for him in Prussia, Marx left Berlin for Cologne, where he edited a radical journal. In this capacity, he was sent a book by a materialist philosopher named Ludwig Feuerbach that dramatically changed his thinking and caused him to break with the Young Hegelians. Reversing Hegel, Feuerbach argued that the spirit of the age was a product of material conditions. His prime example was religion. Human beings create gods, Feuerbach contended, but then they take their own creation as real, worship it, and become dependent on it. Religion, although created by people, becomes separated from them, coming to serve as an idealized compensation for real human misery. (Marx would echo this sentiment in his later notorious comment: "Religion . . . is the opium of the people.")

The implication of the materialist view for cultural sociology is that religion, values, art, ideas, laws, and culture in general are the products of material reality and that we should analyze them as such. As Marx put it, materialists assume that the direction of causality is from earth to heaven, not from heaven to earth. Cultural research, consequently, should move in the same direction.

Historical Materialism

Profoundly influenced by Feuerbach's materialism, Marx soon became impatient with what he considered to be its ignoring of history, and he finally came to the conclusion that Feuerbach was as much of an ivory-tower philosopher as the idealists themselves. It is not enough simply to point out the material basis of illusions, Marx contended in *The German Ideology* (1970). That's like saying, "Gravity is just an illusion," to a man falling from a tall building—in Marx's scornful words, "fighting phrases with phrases."

What Feuerbach didn't see, in Marx's view, was the social and historical roots of the material world. This recognition led to what is known as Marx's historical materialism. A cherry tree, for example, looks solid, a material "given." Yet Marx pointed out that the cherry tree had been brought to Europe from Asia through trade. It wasn't just "there," but had a specific and lengthy history as a product of human labor. Under the terms of historical materialism, the starting point for any analysis was always *homo faber* (man the maker), humans working to sustain themselves through production and reproduction.

Not only material things such as trees, but also consciousness itself is a social product, Marx argued, and this is true of all we think of as culture. Marx claimed that culture, government, religion, politics, and laws are all "superstructure" resting on a base of the material forces of production and their economic foundations. Changes in the base, it follows, bring about changes in superstructure. This argument Marx succinctly put forth in his *Preface to a Contribution to the Critique of Political Economy* (1977, p. 389):

> In the social production of their life, men enter into definite relations that are indispensable and independent of their will, relations of production

which correspond to a definite stage of development of their material productive forces. The sum total of these relations of production constitutes the economic structure of society, the real foundation, on which rises a legal and political superstructure and to which correspond definite forms of social consciousness. The mode of production of material life conditions the social, political and intellectual life process in general. It is not the consciousness of men that determines their being, but, on the contrary, their social being that determines their consciousness.

In talking about revolutionary social change arising from a contradiction between the forces and relations of production, Marx argued that a distinction must be made between material transformation of economic conditions of production and "the legal, political, religious, aesthetic or philosophic—in short, ideological forms in which men become conscious of this conflict and fight it out." In other words, he said, don't judge a period of transformation (or any other period) by its own consciousness, by what people living in the period think and believe, but instead explain the period's consciousness by the contradictions in its material life. The critical analyst should look, therefore, for the social origins of the values or "spirit" of the era.

In this investigation, class interests and antagonisms are the key. As Marx memorably put it, a society's ruling ideas are the ideas of its ruling class. These ideas and values and cultural practices protect their interests and legitimate their position. The ruling class always seeks to justify its preeminent position by making its ideas seem universal ones. But does Marx's theory mean that culture—ideas, values, arts, laws, religion, popular culture—is determined inexorably by a society's material life and the related class antagonisms? It sounds that way, but some have contended that Marx did not envision a simple determinism. Raymond Williams ([1973] 1980), a Marxian cultural analyst, suggested that Marx's "determination" doesn't mean "totally predict," but "setting limits, exerting pressures." He argued that Marxian-inspired analysts should revise their concept of superstructure away from some reflected, reproduced, or dependent content and toward a conception of some related range of cultural practices that are under the influence of, but not strictly determined by, economic conditions.

Marxian theory made the sociological analysis of culture possible by hypothesizing the nature of the linkages between society and culture, the causal direction, and the principles of the relationship between the two. Like all reflection theories, it simplifies the connections indicated by the cultural diamond, but it does offer a substantial theoretical justification for this simplification. Marx's historical materialism has given rise to a rich tradition of cultural research that continues to influence how sociologists think about culture. Let's examine this research with an eye for what is useful in understanding culture today.

Research Directions From the Marxian Tradition

Marxist research always entails a social critique and implicitly or explicitly advocates change. Because cultural objects either enhance or obstruct the understanding of social relations, potentially cultural objects are among the "weapons of criticism" Marx called for and thus can facilitate the historical movement toward socialist revolution. Indeed, this was the key aesthetic criterion for politically committed Marxists.

An especially influential group of thinkers who applied Marxian cultural analysis were the associates of the Frankfurt school. Their background lay in the post-World War I dilemma facing German Marxists: Should they follow Moscow, support the Weimar Republic, or reexamine Marxist theory? The Institute for Social Research in Frankfurt was set up to follow the last of these options. Here assembled Marxist scholars, most from Jewish families, who sought to reconcile their Marxism with the contemporary world. After the Nazis came to power, most of these Frankfurt school associates escaped from Germany, and many moved to Columbia University in the mid-1930s. Max Horkheimer headed this scholarly community, which also included Herbert Marcuse, Theodor Adorno, and Leo Lowenthal.

Members of the Frankfurt school advanced a new critical theory, which organized empirical cultural analysis around a goal of social reformation. In this spirit, they did a great deal of research on authority and mass culture, seeing both as related to the growing helplessness of people in modern society. They criticized mass cultural products as having become mere commodities, commodities that discouraged social protest by making consumers reconciled to their existence. In mounting this critique, the Frankfurt school used the term culture industry to stress the antidemocratic nature of popular culture.

In an interesting example of Marxian cultural analysis, Leo Lowenthal compared biographies of notable Americans found in popular magazines published early in the twentieth century with biographies that appeared in the same magazines during the 1940s ([1944] 1968). Thirty-odd years, Lowenthal discovered, had produced dramatic changes in these stories. The early biographies were usually about inventors, discoverers, or business entrepreneurs, whereas those of the later period were more likely to be about movie stars, sports figures, and other entertainers. Lowenthal concluded that this change represented—reflected—a shift from an economy based on production to one that emphasized consumption and leisure. A related shift had occurred in the amount of detail the biographies contained. Whereas the earlier ones described their subjects as extraordinary, too different from the ordinary run of people to be interested in consumer products, later biographies talked about the ordinary lives of their subjects, including information about the brand of cigarettes the movie star smoked or the type of car the baseball player drove. This, too, reflected the shift from production to consumption values that took place during the century, as small-scale business gave way to giant corporations. As the common people increasingly realized the limits on their ability to succeed, they grew more comfortable with consumption than with production. In other words, Lowenthal concluded, the working-class and middle-class readers no longer believed in the Horatio Alger myth that the early biographies offered.

Music provides another example of the radical critique of popular culture. Theodor Adorno attacked radio music, produced and distributed by the culture industry, with the charge that popular music on the radio, including jazz, is mere repetition that leads its audience to delight in recognition of the familiar, not the challenge of the new. Psychologically, the result is a childlike regression rather than an intellectual awakening. This line of reasoning was typical of the Frankfurt school concerns. Their ultimate fear was that people would become too stupefied by the mass media to protest, or even notice, when their freedoms disappeared.

Meanwhile, in the mid-twentieth century, another theory—functionalism—was proving enormously influential in the sociology of culture and elsewhere. It retained the mirror model of culture while it offered a comprehensive account of human social relations. If Marxism views human social life as a bitter struggle to the death, functionalism views it as a systemic tendency toward harmony. We now need to look at functionalism, so different from Marxist theory yet sharing the reflection model, to see its impact on cultural studies.

Culture and Meaning in Functionalist Sociology

Aristotle's suggestion that culture tells about the kind of thing that happens to human beings may be restated in terms specific to a given society. Thus the culture of the Egyptians tells us about the kinds of things that happen in Egypt, thereby indicating the way Egyptians view their social and natural worlds. In this modified Aristotelian form, reflection theory becomes, for two reasons, a very attractive model for the sociological understanding of culture. First, the idea that "culture reflects society (or social structure)" provides a model of the connection between culture and society and suggests the primary direction of influence. Second, this model allows the use of culture as social evidence.

Both attributes are part and parcel of the functionalist image of a close fit between culture and social structure, at least in a society that is functioning properly. The essence of functionalism is that human societies, to maintain themselves, have concrete needs, and social institutions arise to meet these needs. For example, every society needs to rear and socialize its young, so every society has some regular, institutionalized patterned relationships, called families, that perform this function. A healthy society exists in a state of balance or equilibrium in which institutions are adapted to one another and operate in a system of mutual interdependence to meet the needs of the society. Failures of fit, which all societies experience to some extent, are described as dysfunctional. It follows from this thinking that every social level—the culture, the polity, the economy, the social order—provides input to and receives output from every other level. Every level is adapted to, or reflects, every other level. Thus, culture reflects society just as society reflects culture.

Problems with this simple functionalist version of reflection theory become obvious when we think of specific examples, such as the degree to which popular television shows "reflect" social reality. What about human beings, we might ask, the creators and audiences—the other points of the cultural diamond? The classic functionalist reflection model assumes that these human beings are passive and without interests of their own. And the model does not have a place for the independent influence of the organizations of cultural production—the record companies, church hierarchies, symphonies, art galleries, and so forth.

Even the mirror metaphor is less straightforward than it first appears. From the audience's point of view, for example, is a cultural work a mirror of itself or a window into other people? Here we recall Peter Berger's (1969) point that externalization and internalization are acts not necessarily performed by the same person. And what about the passage of time? The transience of the mirror image seems to conflict with the real permanence many cultural works have shown, a permanence the humanities have suggested is especially significant.

Moreover, the "social evidence" point—the idea that we can read a society directly through its cultural works—is often misleading. We all know, for example, that *Father Knows Best* and other family sitcoms of the 1950s offers a highly skewed portrait of what American family life was actually like during that decade. Cultural objects often idealize certain aspects of social experience, or they emphasize less favorable aspects as a form of social criticism. Or, as Plato recognized, they feature the sensational; few people would suggest that the sexual and criminal shenanigans on the average soap opera "reflect" the way contemporary people really live.

So the pure mirror model, in which social structure and culture are adapted to one another and serve each other's functional needs, seems a bit hard to swallow. More complex functionalist reflection models do exist, however, and they satisfy some of the objections raised here. To take one effective study, art historian Michael Baxandall (1972) suggests a way in which the basic reflection model can represent all of the points and links of the cultural diamond. In his study of fifteenth-century Italian paintings, Baxandall shows how the paintings reflect:

1. *Commercial transactions.* The contract between a painter and his client —the contract would be the horizontal line on our diamond— stipulated the amount of expensive pigments, the extent of gilding, and the proportion of the work that was painted by the master, as opposed to his students.

2. *Changing values.* During the century, the emphasis in the paintings— and what the client was willing to pay for—shifted from pigments to pictorial skill. This reflected changing consumption styles among wealth, specifically a new concern with taste instead of a simple display of wealth, but still was a reflection of class position.

3. *The "period eye."* This important concept refers to the cognitive capacity and style of an era. For example, Baxandall notes the large number of containers, cylinders, and piles of grain or other goods in the paintings. He suggests that these appealed to the knowledge and skills of wealthy merchants, who had to develop great facility at gauging volumes because there were no standard weights and measures at this time. Such merchants were often the painters' clients. Note that Baxandall is giving us a highly sociological definition of *taste*—the conformity between the discriminations of painters and viewers. "If a painting gives us opportunity for exercising a valued skill and rewards our virtuosity with a sense of worthwhile insights about that painting's organization, we tend to enjoy it: it is to our taste" (p. 34). Sociologist Ann Swidler (1986) refers to culture as a "toolkit" of symbols, repertoires, practices, knowledge, recipes,

and ways of doing things. Baxandall's concept of taste is a matter of matching the toolkit of the painter with that of the viewer, or in other words, finding the shared vision of their "period eyes."

In this reflection argument, culture is not a direct reflection of the social world, but rather is mediated through the minds of human beings. Renaissance Italian paintings reflect the social experience that has produced a certain way of seeing things, a period eye composed of a "stock of patterns, categories and methods of inference; training in a range of representational conventions; and experience drawn from the environment, in what are plausible ways of visualizing what we have incomplete information about" (Baxandall, 1972, p. 32). And not only the general social experience of fifteenth-century Italians is reflected, but also that of the specific class of men—and they were virtually all men—who produced and bought the paintings. At the same time, the analysis is recognizably functionalist (although as an art historian, Baxandall probably would not use the term). From the position of social structure, the rising merchant class requires a way to demonstrate its wealth and to indicate its participation in aristocratic patterns of behavior such as art patronage. From the position of culture, painters require buyers who understand and approve of what they see. The merchants and the paintings, respectively representing social structure and culture here, were functionally adapted to one another.

Although a complex reflection model is more satisfactory than the simple culture-reflects-society view, questions remain. How do cultural works remain effective over space and time? Twentieth-century people don't have a fifteenth-century period eye, yet we still respond to the art of the Italian Renaissance. Somehow, new meanings must be created, meanings not dependent on the original period eye, and the reflection model does not help us understand where these come from. Another question would be, Why are some "realities" reflected and not others? Culture is clearly selective in the way that mirrors are not.

Both of these problems come through clearly in the newspaper article "Jerusalem billboards are cultural mosaic" (*Chicago Tribune*, Feb. 9, 1992). The article describes the 290 billboards scattered around the city's Jewish sector that carry ads, public announcements, death notices, political slogans, and posters for concerts and causes. Such billboards, proclaims the anonymous writer for the Associated Press, "reflect the religious, political and ethnic mosaic that makes up the Holy City."

Yet although the article unhesitatingly frames its discussion in a functionalist-reflection model, the text denies this cozy fit between Jerusalem's social structure and this "cultural mosaic." The poster culture speaks only to and about Jews; according to the article, "the Arab public prefers to send its messages through its newspapers or political slogans daubed on walls." Because the billboards are controlled by Jerusalem's municipal government, one might well wonder whether Arab preferences are the reason they don't use such billboards. Notices on the boards can be aggressively chauvinistic. One notice urges "the Zionist-religious public" to settle in a Jewish housing complex being constructed on the Arab side of the city, while another calls Israel to "RESCUE THE LAND AND THE NATION" by rebuilding the biblical temple on the hill now occupied by the city's main mosque. So while the article speaks of reflection, its content shows the cultural mirror to be imperfect indeed: The billboards are selective (Jewish concerns only), they represent the "period eye" of only one portion of the population, and they have very different meaning to passing Arabs. With its emphasis on adaptation and systemic stability, the functionalist reflection model obscures the opposition and conflict that the reporter actually witnesses.

Reservations about the mirror metaphor, especially in its functionalist version, have led some people to suggest that culture is more a reflection "on" than a reflection "of." Culture may be a reflection, not in the literal mirror sense, but in sense of a "consideration of some subject matter, idea, or purpose often with a view to understanding or accepting it or seeing it in its right relations" (*Webster's Third New International Dictionary*, 1986, p. 1908, definition 7a). Through culture, in other words, human beings may reflect on their individual and social experience. Such a transformation of the reflection idea, although safe, is not very sociologically appealing.

Let us pause here to review where we've been. At the opening of this chapter we saw how culture provides the meanings that human beings find essential. It therefore followed that a sociological understanding of culture would attempt to connect cultural meanings with the social world. A standard approach, rooted in Platonic and Aristotelian cultural theory, is to envision culture as reflecting the social world. Both functionalist and Marxist theories of culture employ the reflection model. Now we look at a quite different analysis of cultural meaning that has the effect of reversing the direction of reflection. This is the cultural theory of Max Weber.

Culture and Meaning in Weberian Sociology

Both the functionalist and the Marxian version of reflection theory recognize that culture and social structure exert mutual influence on one another but both tend to emphasize a causal arrow that goes in one direction: Society (or social structure, or the economic base, or class relations) causes (or determines, or shapes, or influences) culture. In terms of the cultural diamond, the arrow generally points downward. Yet if human beings require meaning to organize their lives, then culture, as a bearer of meanings, must make something happen in the social world. The arrow must point upward as well.

The social scientist most known for emphasizing this other direction of causality is Max Weber (1864-1920), the German sociologist mentioned in Chapter 1. Like his contemporary, Durkheim, and Marx a bit earlier, Weber tried to understand the modern world, especially industrial, capitalist society. Weber did not think that culture simply caused social structure. He knew that the influence worked both ways, and in his writing on religion and economic life he took pains to emphasize that he was looking at "only one side" of the causal relationship and not claiming that religion caused capitalism. What interested Weber was the extent to which religion participated in the formation and expansion of the spirit of capitalism. He sought correlations between religious beliefs on the one hand and practical behavior and ethics on the other in order to see how a religious movement might have influenced material culture. In his masterpiece *The Protestant Ethic and the Spirit of Capitalism* ([1904-5] 1958), Weber made a powerful case for the influence of cultural meanings on economic life itself, and thus on the social world.

The Anxious Protestants and the World They Built

Weber began *The Protestant Ethic and the Spirit of Capitalism* by noting how the West is unique in many respects: in its specialized science and arts, its highly trained officials, its rational law, and most especially its capitalist economic system involving "the pursuit of profit, and forever *renewed* profit, by means of continuous, rational, capitalistic enterprise" (p. 17). Human greed is nothing new; there has always been desire for acquisition, and every society has had its capitalists. Unique to the West, according to Weber, is the capitalist organization of human labor, the separation of business from the household, and the dominance of rational bookkeeping. The central problem, then, is not the origin of capitalism itself, but rather the ascendancy of bourgeois capitalism with its rational organization of free labor. Putting the problem another way, Weber claimed to be interested in origins of the bourgeoisie—those sober middle-class capitalists—and their peculiarities. The side of the causal chain he wished to explore was how an economic spirit, or the ethos (distinguishing character) of an economic system, reflected a set of religious ideas.

Weber began with an observation: Everywhere in Europe, Protestants were drawn to commerce, business, and skilled labor far more than were Catholics; they were, in other words, overrepresented in capitalist economic activities. Weber considered the spirit of capitalism as involving an ethic or duty, particularly one's duty in a calling, as exemplified by such aphorisms of Benjamin Franklin as "Time is money." In Franklin's writings, Weber (p. 49) finds a mixture of profit seeking and rational calculation (e.g., "After industry and frugality, nothing contributes more to the raising of a young man in the world than punctuality and justice in all his dealings; therefore never keep borrowed money an hour beyond the time you promised, lest a disappointment shut up your friend's purse for ever") a type of thinking that seems unique to Western capitalism.

This spirit of capitalism stood in sharp contrast to the traditional attitude, whereby people work only to live as they are accustomed to doing. Those under capitalism work incessantly for profits, going well beyond their needs and driven by a "time is money" type of self-imposed motivation. The ideal type of capitalist was not a hedonist who enjoyed wealth, but an ascetic: "He gets nothing out of his wealth for himself, except the irrational sense of having done his job well" (p. 71). If the spirit of capitalism can't be explained by the desire for luxury, neither can it be explained by material conditions. Weber compared fifteenth-century Florence, where capitalism was advanced but lacked the distinctive later "spirit," to the eighteenth-century Pennsylvania of Franklin, which had more of the spirit than it did capitalism itself. What was the "background of ideas" that made activity directed toward profit into a morally charged vocation?

The answer lies in two Protestant religious ideas: the calling and predestination. Martin Luther's conception of the calling—the particular vocation to which God has "called" every man and woman—gave a moral justification to worldly activity. This interpretation was in contrast with Catholicism, wherein such activity was morally neutral at best. Luther stressed that Providence has assigned each person a place in God's scheme, and a specific job to do. Pursuit of one's vocation, one's calling, is a way of serving God.

The idea of a calling might encourage pious Protestants to work hard, but it would not make them endlessly pursue profits without stopping to enjoy their gains. This pattern of action came from another strand in Protestant theology, that involving predestination. As theorized by John Calvin, predestination is the belief that, at the beginning of time, God had destined every individual for heaven or hell; there was nothing people could do to change their destinies. According to Calvin, God is unknowable, and his decrees incomprehensible; He has decided everything, and one must trust in His justice without question.

Such a harsh doctrine, Weber reasoned, would produce a feeling of unprecedented inner loneliness for those who believed in it. "In what was for the man of the age of the Reformation the most important thing in life, his eternal salvation, he was forced to follow his path alone to meet a destiny which had been decreed for him from eternity" (Weber, 1904, p. 104). No person, no sacraments, no church, not even God could help. How was such a religion bearable? Weber said that the Calvinists responded to the psychological pressure by becoming obsessed with seeking hints regarding whether they were destined for salvation. Their clergy made two suggestions: (1) It was one's duty to consider oneself saved (if a person worried openly about going to hell, he or she probably would!), and (2) one might gain self-confidence in one's heavenly destination through worldly activity. Protestants could bolster their conviction of salvation through good works, self-control, and purposeful activity. In contrast to monastic withdrawal, such lives were ones of what Weber called "inner-worldly asceticism," in which Calvinists enacted their religious beliefs in the workshops, markets, and households in which they lived their lives.

Weber saw the Puritan as a man concerned with monitoring his own state of grace, engaged in endless moral bookkeeping and the methodical Christianization of his entire life. He labored hard in his calling, but did not spend or enjoy his profits. If successful, he just worked harder; he could never rest, for complacency might be a sign of damnation. Such a pattern of behavior had two results: (1) It built up the capital of those who practiced it (all of those unspent profits were available for investment) and (2) it developed an attitude toward hard work as a "good thing" for its own sake that was foreign to the traditional assumption that work was just a means to an end. The spirit of capitalism lasted long after the particular religious beliefs themselves (e.g., a strict belief in predestination) had atrophied. Indeed, Weber saw the spirit of capitalism operating in his own day, and in many respects it persists in ours as well.

The Cultural Switchman

In *The Protestant Ethic and the Spirit of Capitalism*, Weber showed how a set of religious ideas influenced the way people worked, spent their money, and ordered their economic lives. The result of a particular religion-based form of economic behavior helped give rise to the Western form of capitalism that has dominated the world economy for three centuries. Thus, this "side of the causal chain" maps onto our cultural diamond as the way that culture causes, or influences, or is reflected in the social world.

Weber himself did not want to deny that people pursued their material interests—to this extent he endorsed Marx's *homo faber* as a starting point—but he contended that their ideas, their cultures, shaped just how they pursued these interests. In a famous metaphor, he once compared the role of culture to that of a railroad switchman: "Not ideas, but material and ideal interests, directly govern men's conduct. Yet very frequently the 'world images' that have been created by 'ideas' have, like switchmen, determined the tracks along which action has been pushed by the dynamic of interest" (1946, p. 280). Thus the Calvinists had material interests (earning a living) and ideal interests (salvation). A set of religious world images involving a calling and predestination set the tracks along which they pursued these interests by making these pursuits meaningful. And along those tracks Western capitalists and workers still run their economic lives.

Like functionalism and Marxism, the Weberian model that social action reflects cultural meanings has directed much sociological research, especially attempts to explain broad social change. For example, when Jack Goldstone (1991) sought to explain the wave of revolutions that convulsed Europe and Asia in the seventeenth and eighteenth centuries, he showed that sudden population increases triggered a set of factors—government incapacity, elite conflict, popular discontent—that led to state breakdown and rebellion. But then a new puzzle emerged: Why did these structural factors lead to revolution in the West (England, France) but not in the East (the Ottoman Empire, China). What about the state breakdowns—such as those of the Ming-Qing transition in China and the Ottoman crisis—that lead not to revolutions but to the restoration of traditional forms of authority?

Goldstone found the answer in Weber's cultural switchman model. The Western religious tradition was linear and eschatological; when a change occurred, such as the coming of the Messiah, it was once-and-for-all. Revolutionary action made sense in this meaning system, for history has a direction, total transformations are possible, and things can get better. Eastern religions, on the other hand, view history as cyclical, not linear. This way of thinking did not "switch" political and economic grievances toward revolutionary action, but encouraged a return to previous forms of authority. This example demonstrates the ability of cultural explanations to complement structural ones, and the utility of the "cultural switchman" line of reasoning.

The reflection model—whether we emphasize the causal direction going from culture to social world or the reverse—is most persuasive when used to reveal correspondences between society and culture that were previously hidden. In other words, although the mirror metaphor can be misleading if it is taken too literally and if it excludes other points of the cultural diamond, it can nevertheless reveal significant parallels between cultural objects and their social world. An exemplary reflection study of Chinese religion offers a final illustration of this point.

Gods, Ghosts, and Ancestors: A Case Study of Reflection Theory

In his study of peasant religion in Taiwan, Arthur Wolf (1974) maintains that Chinese religion "mirrors the social landscape of its adherents" (p. 131). He supports his reflection model by showing how traditional Chinese religion presents its followers with three types of supernatural beings:

1. Gods, who are bureaucratically organized in an administrative hierarchy—so much so, in fact, that some gods seem to be more positions than individuals—and who are concerned with overall social well-being.
2. Ancestors, who are concerned with the well-being of kin groups. Unlike the gods, the ancestors exist in a relationship of mutual dependence with humans; for example, if people make sacrifices to their ancestors, the ancestors are obliged to help them.
3. Ghosts, who are dead strangers, not one's ancestors, and who are despised and feared because they are threatening beings who must be placated or else they will cause trouble. If their living descendants do not care for them (one person's ancestors are another person's ghosts, of course), ghosts will be malicious, and in any case all are potentially dangerous.

How does this tripartite pantheon reflect the traditional Chinese social structure? Taking the point of view of a peasant living in a rural village, which was the situation of the vast majority of Chinese, Wolf suggests that the mightiest god reflects a human emperor, remote and omnipotent. Lesser gods reflect the Mandarins: the imperial bureaucrats and the various tax collectors and other government officials who had the power to conscript into the army, seize produce, and otherwise disrupt the villagers' lives. Ancestors reflect senior members of one's own lineage, the family's fathers and mothers; in a sense, the dead and the living elders formed a single continuum. And ghosts reflect strangers and outsiders, the potential bandits or other unknown figures, coming from beyond the village's local area, whom Chinese peasants feared. This three-part structure further reflected the dual social relations of *sin* and *kui*. Schematically, Wolf's reflection model looks like Figure 2-3.

Figure 2-3

Chinese Religion Reflecting Chinese Society

Supernatural Order	Social Landscape	Social Relations
Gods	Mandarins	*Sin:* productive social relations; positive, immaterial, celestial aspect of human soul
Ancestors	Lineage, senior members	
Ghosts	Strangers, outsiders	*Kui:* social forces that are dangerous; negative, material, terrestrial aspect of soul

SOURCE: Adapted from Wolf, 1974

Wolf's account of Chinese religion is a well-reasoned example of the culture-reflects-social-structure line of thinking, which still dominates how we—as sociologists and as sensible human beings—view the relationship between culture and society. In spite of the refinements to this theory we have examined in this chapter, you will encounter many other simple reflection arguments or assumptions in the popular media, as well as in the sociological literature. In fact, once you are alert to the reflection model, you will hear and see it everywhere. In a typical example, the *Chicago Tribune* reported that a 3-year-old newspaper for Irish and Irish Americans called the *Irish Voice* was giving its 65-year-old rival, the *Irish Echo*, some stiff competition (Dorning, 1993). The *Voice* has taken a social activist position on such issues as the controversy over gays marching in New York's St. Patrick's Day parade. Says the *Tribune*, "the *Voice*, much like the openly gay marchers, reflects a new Irish community in New York and elsewhere in America, one enlarged by a generation of immigrants who left their economically depressed homeland during the 1980s." Because this new wave was more urban and educated than earlier Irish immigrants had been, and also more likely to be illegal, the *Voice* "has given expression" to their concerns in its advocacy of progressive causes, its "Dear Bridget" advice column dealing with such issues as live-in lovers and single motherhood, and its "Green Card" column offering tips on immigration laws. Compared with the *Voice*, the staid *Echo* looks like a "parish newsletter." Here we have a straightforward reflection argument that could be set right on our cultural diamond, arrow pointing downward: A change in the social world, specifically a new wave of immigrants with distinctive demographic characteristics, finds itself reflected (or expressed) in the emergence of a new newspaper.

Academic reflection assumptions are equally commonplace. In his study of designs used on pieces of pottery turned up by archaeologists, J. L. Fischer (1970) shows how artistic styles "reflect" social stratification; repetitive designs with simple elements are associated with egalitarian societies, whereas designs integrating unlike elements are products of more hierarchical societies. Such an account is one more use of the basic reflection model, which we have seen in the work of Lowenthal, Baxandall, and Goldstone. All such studies reveal the reflection assumption: Decorative design, like Chinese religion or Irish newspapers, reflects the social structure of its origin—or, social change reflects cultural assumptions. As we have seen, an unthinking acceptance of this reflection model can get us into trouble, but the basic premise of some form of culture/social world correspondence is usually a sound one.

Summary

In this chapter, we have considered the relationship between culture and meaning. We have seen how human beings require meaningful orientation for their lives and how culture provides such orientation. We have looked at the origin and history of reflection theory. We have looked at several modern sociological theories of how culture, as a bearer of meaning, connects with the social world. Some of these theories, such as Marx's, perpetuate a classical reflection model whereby culture reflects social structure like a mirror. Others, notably that of Weber, emphasize how social structures respond to cultural meanings.

If we return to the cultural diamond for a moment, we notice that all of these theories have one thing in common, as Figure 2-4 indicates: They concentrate on the vertical axis of the diamond. The left point of cultural

Figure 2-4

Reflection and the Cultural Diamond

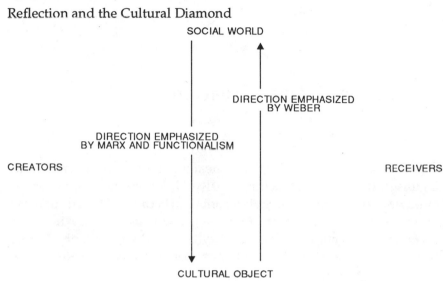

creation, the right point of cultural reception, and the five links beyond the vertical axis are virtually ignored.

For all their power and plausibility, the theories that concentrate on relating cultural meaning to the social world downplay the role of human agency, of active human beings who produce the ideas, the theologies, the art, the media, and the popular culture that are the vessels of meaning. Similarly, these theories downplay the thoughts and actions of those who receive the cultural messages, who interpret, accept, or reject some of the suggested meanings. In this de-emphasis they may be said to be incomplete. Accordingly, in the following two chapters we concentrate on the facets of the cultural diamond that have thus far been neglected: the social basis for cultural creation, production, and reception.

3

Culture as a Social Creation

We have seen that culture possesses meaning. Cultural objects are meaningful to human beings living in a social world; conversely, the social world, otherwise random and chaotic, is meaningful because of the cultural lens through which people view it. But pressing questions remain: Who makes specific cultural objects? How are they endowed with meaning? What types of creators and creative operations does the left point of our cultural diamond represent?

As a cultural creator, consider Bessie Smith. Regarded in her own time as the "Empress of the Blues" and since as a singularly important figure in American music, Smith was the woman who established the "classic blues" style in the 1920s. Classic may seem an odd term for blues singing (odder still is the fact that it never is applied to male singers), but this specific musical form is African-American country blues rooted in the Mississippi Delta combined with a vaudeville style of showmanship and tinged with jazz. With her extraordinary vocal gifts, flamboyant lifestyle, and great popularity, Bessie Smith seems to fit the standard image of exceptional individuals who create cultural objects by shaping and bending symbolic expressive forms to their will. This creative-artist-as-genius view holds that Bessie Smith took a form of Negro folk singing, polished it, and delivered it with a smooth sophistication to audiences a long way from the Delta. Accounts of Smith's early talent (she made her musical debut at the Ivory Theater in Chattanooga at the age of nine), domineering personality (she refused to let any other blues singers appear on the bill with her), and premature death (she died in an auto accident in Mississippi at 39; one popular, but probably incorrect, story has it that she bled to death because the hospital for whites would not treat her) support this story of individual cultural creation.

The singer who distills the experience of her people into the blues, the reformer who leads a social movement based on a new vision of social justice, the artist working feverishly in a lonely studio, the prophet with burning eyes who brings a message from God, the animator who dreams up a character called Mickey Mouse, the poet who transforms the beauty of nature into a simple haiku, the praise-singer who comes up with an innovative song to celebrate the chief—all of these figures we recognize as cultural creators. In moments of inspiration, these individuals create something altogether new, something moving, entertaining, brilliant, and often either profoundly disturbing or delightful. Such gifted people—the van Goghs and Bessie Smiths, the Disneys and Jeremiahs—change the cultural world in which human beings live.

So the answer to the question, Where does culture come from? at first seems to be "from the efforts of individual geniuses." But this individualistic answer seems to work best for individual cultural objects such as a blues style or a haiku. What about culture in the broader sense of a "historically transmitted pattern of meaning"? It is harder to think of culture at this level as "coming from" anywhere. It seems always to have been there.

Sociology suggests an alternative to both the unsatisfying "it has always been that way" view at one extreme and the unsociological "individual genius" view on the other. This alternative posits that culture and cultural works are collective, not individual, creations. We can best understand specific cultural objects—the haiku, Jeremiah's prophesy, Bessie Smith's singing—by seeing them not as unique to their creators but as the fruits of collective production, fundamentally social in their genesis. In this chapter we explore the background and implications of the sociological approach to cultural creation. In the following pages, we try to indicate how a fuller picture of Bessie Smith's singing emerges when viewed as a collective product, the result of Smith's concrete location in a particular social world, a context with competing cultural traditions and individual opportunities, organizations, and markets.

This view of culture as a social product originates in the work of Emile Durkheim on religion. We begin the chapter, therefore, by reviewing Durkheim's analysis and by considering what happens when we follow his suggestion to view culture as collective representation. We then examine four contemporary sociological approaches to the collective production of culture: symbolic interactionism, the study of subcultures, research on whether cultural changes precede or follow social changes, and the social basis for creative innovations. As we proceed, we return often to the case of Bessie Smith to see how a sociological understanding of cultural creation can enrich our understanding of her music.

Durkheim and the Social Production of Culture

Emile Durkheim (1864-1917) was a French sociologist working in the late nineteenth and early twentieth centuries. Along with Marx and Weber, he is considered to be the third "founding father" of the discipline of sociology. Like these other two, he tried to understand how modern societies worked.

To these founders of sociology, as to modernist poets and artists such as William Butler Yeats, the modern world seemed fractured, divided, increasingly unglued (Yeats, 1956, p. 184):

> *Things fall apart, the centre cannot hold;*
> *Mere anarchy is loosed upon the world . . .*

Social chaos—"mere anarchy"—seemed a real possibility. Over and over, the question, What can hold society together? troubled thinkers of the early twentieth century.[1] Durkheim investigated everything from suicide to religion to systems of education to science to sociological methods with this central question in mind. In his theory of collective representation, he thought he had found the answer.

The Problem of Modern Social Life

In modern life, Durkheim observed, people can be sorted in many ways: They have different occupations, different fields of knowledge and expertise, different beliefs, different life experiences. Durkheim compared this to an earlier, less differentiated social state, which he called mechanical solidarity, wherein people were bound together because their lives were similar. In simpler times, he reasoned, each member of a society did the same type of work (e.g., farming), followed the same religion, raised and educated their children, thought and believed and hoped and feared in pretty much the same way. Each member of the society could say confidently, "My people do this" or "My people believe this." The shared beliefs and understandings of a people constituted their collective consciousness, and this collective consciousness governed their thoughts, attitudes, and practices.

Change came when societies grew in size and density and people began to specialize. The most obvious form of specialization is the different types

---

[1]Nigerian novelist Chinua Achebe (1958) used Yeats's words—*Things Fall Apart* —as the title for his novel about the destruction of the traditional Igbo way of life under British colonialism. Achebe, like Yeats and Durkheim, was concerned about what happens when rapid social change undermines a society.

of work people do, but institutional specialization occurred as well. In the past, for example, teaching the young what they needed to know, performing religious rituals, and making the transitions of birth and death took place within the family, and the society as a whole exerted strong pressures against deviation. Modern institutions—schools, mosques, hospitals—separate these life processes from the family, and from one another as well. Durkheim asked, just as we still ask: Under such conditions of specialization and differentiation, how can such societies hold together?

Durkheim considered a number of possible answers to this question. At times he stressed the need for people to exchange with one another, a state he called organic solidarity; in effect, the farmer exchanges his produce with the teacher who, in return, educates his children, just as the organs of the body exchange with one another. At other times he proposed professional associations as a future source of cohesion. Although he never settled on a single solution to his problem, Durkheim believed that every society must have some kind of collective representation, some tie-that-binds that demonstrated to the society's members that they were indeed connected to one another.

Social Bonds: The Role of Religion

Durkheim's search for collective representation and how it worked led him to take a close look at religion, which he viewed as the most fundamental bond among people of earlier times. His magnificent study of the social production of religion, *The Elementary Forms of the Religious Life* ([1915] 1965), was to be his most influential work in cultural studies. Durkheim wrote this work toward the end of his career, when his thinking had changed from an early emphasis on structural influences on social behavior to a greater concern with culture and meaning. In *The Elementary Forms of the Religious Life*, Durkheim looked at what he regarded as the most primitive forms of religion—the totemism of Australian aborigines and certain Native American groups. Why study primitive religion if his interest was in human society today? Durkheim began with a functionalist postulate: A human institution such as religion cannot rest upon error or superstition; instead, it responds to a profound human need. Consequently, he saw three reasons for studying primitive religions: (1) to see religion's "constituent elements," or simplest forms, (2) to find the fundamentals of all religions, and (3) to find the human need that caused religious belief and practice.

Durkheim's analysis of religion is based on four key ideas: (1) collective representation, (2) the distinction between the sacred and the profane, (3) the origins of the sacred, and (4) the social consequences of religion. We will examine these both to see how his argument develops and to comprehend the consequences of his thinking about religion for cultural sociology more generally.

First, Durkheim argued, religion is the basis for all categories of thinking, and religion and categories of thinking alike are "collective representations which express collective realities" (p. 22). How does he make this argument? Human beings, he pointed out, cannot conceive of time and space independent of socially agreed-upon divisions, even though we know they are arbitrary and not natural. The seven-day week, for example, is a social convention of Western societies, one we know to be artificial (in Nigeria, the Igbo have a four-day week), and yet it is impossible to think of time without resorting to this convention. Durkheim asserted that all categories of thought, all essential ideas, are social. Human beings are "double"—we possess an individual biological component and a shared social component that is our participation in a collective consciousness—and our categories of thought, including our sense of the religious, come from that second social component. Hence, religion and culture are collective representations.

But how does the society, the collective, make its presence felt within us? Durkheim answered this question in the next two steps of his argument. He started by asking, What do all religions have in common? The answer is not that they all believe in some supernatural or divine being; Buddhism doesn't, for example. There is a simpler answer: All religious beliefs divide the world into sacred and profane. Now there is nothing special about the nature of what is sacred; virtually anything can fit this category. As was said in Chapter 1, bread, the homeliest of European and American foods, becomes sacred in the Christian communion. Similarly, Native American and Australian groups sanctify such animals as snakes, insects, and carrion-eaters that other cultures despise. What characterizes the sacred is rather that it is absolutely separated from the profane and cannot be approached with impunity—we are reminded of this in the Biblical story of Uzzah, who touched the ark of God and was killed on the spot[2]—and the core of religion lies in this separation. "A religion is a unified system of beliefs and practices relative to sacred things, that is to say, things set apart and forbidden—beliefs and practices which unite

---

[2]In II Samuel 6, David and the people of Israel are bringing the ark to Jerusalem on an oxcart when one of the oxen stumbles. Uzzah grabs the ark to keep it from falling, thereby violating the prohibition against touching it. "And the anger of the Lord was kindled against Uzzah; and God smote him there because

into one single moral community called a Church, all those who adhere to them" (Durkheim, [1915] 1965, p. 62).

Durkheim traced our sense of the sacred by looking at totems, which are central to "elementary forms" of religion. He pointed out that many simple societies are organized around clans, which are kinship groups distinguished by having names like "the kangaroo clan" or "the people of the white eagle." Each such name represents the clan's totem, which serves as the emblem of the clan; this image or representation of the clan is put on its property and the bodies of its members, especially when the clan gathers together. More than just a name or emblem, however, the totem is sacred, and all sorts of ritual prohibitions surround it, a taboo against eating it, for example. These tribal peoples base their entire cosmologies, their classifications of human beings and nature, on the totem, thus imposing a sacred/profane structure on the entire universe.

Up to this point, Durkheim has argued that the sacred/profane distinction organizes and classifies all social and natural beings and that this distinction can be seen in its most elementary form in the totemic religions of tribal people. But where do such people get the idea that the totemic emblem is sacred? Clearly, not from the object itself, for the totem is often a rather lowly animal. Durkheim's answer to this question is the heart of his cultural analysis. The totem, he suggested, symbolizes two things: the totemic principal (or, we would say, god) and the clan. "So if it is once the symbol of the god and of the society, is that not because the god and the society are only one?" (p. 236). The god of the clan, in other words, is the clan itself.

How does Durkheim justify this conclusion? Society, he suggested, arouses a sensation of divinity in human beings through (1) its power, its control over us, shown in its ability to cause or inhibit our actions without regard for individual utility, and (2) its positive force, the "strengthening and vivifying action of society." When a member of society is in moral harmony with his comrades, "he has more confidence, courage, and boldness in action, just like the believer who thinks that he feels the regard of his god turned graciously toward him. [Society] thus produces, as it were, a perpetual sustenance of our moral nature" (p. 242). People think this moral support must be due to some external cause, some force always represented with religious symbols, and they respond to the force with

he put forth his hand to the ark; and he died there beside the ark of God." (6:7). Even David was upset by what God had done. The natural human reaction ("Uzzah was only trying to help!" we want to protest) is secondary, however, to the absolute against profaning the sacred by touching it.

respect and awe. It seems as if there were two sorts of reality—that associated with the force (sacred), and that associated with the everyday (profane).

Using the example of Australian clans, Durkheim shows how people awaken to a sense of religious force. The aborigines, like most hunter-gatherers, experience their lives as having two phases: times of scattered wandering in groups, and times of gathering for a ceremony called the corroboree. In the first phase, which is normal everyday life, things are "uniform, languishing, and dull." But during the corroboree, people come together to sing, dance around the fire, enjoy a sexual freedom that is normally forbidden, and celebrate until they drop from exhaustion. In such a gathering, life is emotional, people are animated by powerful forces and passions, and each sentiment is echoed back by another until the energy and exuberance grow like an avalanche. Durkheim referred to this stage as one of "collective effervescence." When taken up by such collective effervescence, people feel that they are not themselves or that they are, almost literally, "carried away."

Because their lives have such very different phases—the routine everyday and the effervescent corroboree—the aborigines believe they participate in two separate worlds: the profane, which is flat and dull, and the sacred, which is charged with energy and excitement. Thus is born the religious idea of the sacred and the profane and the absolute separation between them. And why does the force felt during sacred time get associated with the totem? Durkheim reasoned that because the totem is the clan name, totemic emblems are all around during the gathering of the clan. Because of its visibility during these times, the totem comes to represent both the scene and the strong emotions felt. It becomes a collective representation.

Therefore, Durkheim concluded, the rational folks who equate religion with superstition are wrong. The religious force is real enough, but the source of the force is not what the believer thinks: "The believer is not deceived when he believes in the existence of a moral power upon which he depends and from which he receives all that is best in himself: this power exists, it is society" (p. 257). The religious force comes not from a totem or god, but from the experience of the social. Religion, therefore, is the system of ideas by which people represent their society. And because religion is the source of the classifications through which we apprehend the world, all of human culture becomes a representation of the social.

Culture as Collective Representation

Durkheim's analysis of religion further suggests that all cultural objects are collective representations. They represent not just a particular society but social experience itself. We recognize the functionalist thread here: Groups and societies need collective representations of themselves to inspire sentiments of unity and mutual support, and culture fulfills this need.

The idea that culture represents society is one we have seen before in reflection theories. Rather than assuming a straight reflection, however, Durkheim's analysis shows a more complex picture of how cultural objects, such as religious beliefs, can represent our experience of the social in all its force. Culture, including religion, is a collective representation in two senses. First, the cultural objects we began with—a painting, a social movement, a prophecy, an idea, a blues song—are not simply created by an individual touched by genius or inspired by God. Instead, they are produced by people bound to other people, people who are working, celebrating, suffering, loving, like the clan members in Australia. Second, in their cultural products, people represent their experiences of work, joy, pain, and love. Durkheim's cultural theory gives us the social mechanism where-by cultural creators produce, in Wallace Stevens's words, "a tune beyond us, yet ourselves."

The implication for sociological research would be that if one were to try to understand a certain group of people, one would look for the expressive forms through which they represent themselves to themselves (and to others, although this function would be secondary in importance). A business organization, a youth gang, a nation, a family—any identifiable social group will develop collective representations through which it demonstrates its collective solidarity to itself and others. The sociologist can come at this collective representation process from the other direction, from the analysis of a particular cultural object, as well; if we were to try to understand a cultural object, we would look for how it is used by some group as representing that group. The object need not be a straight reflection of any trait of the group, anymore than the grasshopper totem reflects anything particularly grasshopper-like about the clan in question, but it would be a representation of the group's membership and collective experience.

What would it mean, then, to say that Bessie Smith's blues were collective representations? It would imply that even songs about individual pain represent group experience, in this case that of Negroes in the American South during the early twentieth century. For example, many of her songs tell of losing a man. On one level, this theme could be regarded as the expression of the universal problem of lost love; at another, personal level, it could express a very specific problem of how one woman lost one man at one particular time. On an intermediate level, however, a social representation occurs as well, and this specific representation speaks to the difficulties of sustained relationships among impoverished blacks in the rural South. "Frosty Morning Blues," for example, begins, "Did you ever wake up on a frosty morning and discover your good man gone?" Sharecroppers living in unheated shacks—and this was the condition of most Southern blacks during the time Bessie Smith was singing—would have been loath to leave their beds on cold mornings; their shared experience of this common misery lends a collective weight to the individual's particular misery of being abandoned. This collective understanding of the pleasures of warm beds and the pain of cold floors "on a frosty morning" can be said to "strengthen and vivify," in Durkheim's language, even the bawdy development of the frosty morning metaphor: "Oh my damper is down and my fire ain't burning and a chill's all around my bed." Both the humor and the pathos of the song, and of Bessie Smith's blues more generally, represent the social world in which they originated.

The Collective Production of Culture

Applying Durkheim's insights constitutes what we call the collective production approach to cultural meanings. This approach tries to take away the mystery about the creation of art, ideas, beliefs, religion, and culture in general by revealing the many social activities, such as interaction, cooperation, organization, and contestation, involved in the formation of what we designate as cultural objects. If culture is a collective representation, as Durkheim argued, then the collective production approach investigates the nuts-and-bolts of just how the collectivity goes about representing itself.

Collective production theory has two sides. One involves the interactions among people and how these interactions themselves generate culture. This version of collective production theory is rooted in the branch of social psychology known as symbolic interactionism. In the remainder of this chapter we look at such interactions and how they work on both the small group level and the broader societal level. The second type of collective production looks less at interactions and more at the organization of cultural producers and consumers, including such things as culture industries, distribution mechanisms, and the markets for cultural products. These studies, generated by what is usually called the production-of-culture school and rooted in organizational and economic sociology, will be examined in Chapter 4.

Symbolic Interactionism

Most branches of social theory assume certain things as given. For example, although we might try to explain how the norms of a society constrain its members to act in one way and not another, the norm itself—say, the norm of apologizing if you bump into someone—is taken as a given. Or we might examine certain roles, such as the role of a teacher or of a mother, to see how they are enacted, but the roles themselves are largely taken for granted. Symbolic interactionism is concerned with how people actively construct and learn their norms and roles. The basic insight of the interactionists is that the human self is not a preexisting Platonic form, but is shaped through social interaction. An early theorist of this school was Charles Horton Cooley, who coined the term "looking-glass self" ([1902] 1964). According to Cooley, an interaction has three phases: (1) the self imagines another's response to his or her appearance, (2) the self imagines the other person's judgment of the action, and (3) the self has an emotional reaction, such as of pride or shame, to that judgment. For example, a little girl is running and bumps into a boy in her play group. The girl observes the boy's expression of pain and anger, and she imagines that he thinks her clumsy or thoughtless. She understands his probable judgment of her action (he may say, "Hey, watch out" or give her a scornful look), and she responds emotionally (she feels embarrassed or ashamed at having hurt him or provoked his anger). Through such interactions, the norm of apologizing when accidentally bumping into someone else gets established, for the apology constitutes a second interaction sequence to restore the social harmony that has been disrupted by the first.

All social learning does not take place through two-person interactions, of course. George Herbert Mead (1934) pointed out that the developing child first learns to take the role of another person. This is the "play" stage; the child plays at being a teacher or plays with an imaginary friend. Later comes the more complicated "game" stage, wherein the child learns to take on and take into account a variety of other roles. Mead used the analogy of the baseball game: The runner has to know what the shortstop is likely to do, what the fielder will try to do, and so forth. Children move from play to games as they develop more complex responses to those with whom they do or might interact. Ultimately, the child learns to take into account the response of the generalized other, which is Mead's term for the society—Mead calls it "the organized community or social group which gives to the individual his unity of self" (p. 154)—with which the individual always implicitly interacts. This generalized other is the source of morality, and children are socialized into understanding what it expects. "It is in the form of the generalized other that the social process influences the behavior of the individuals involved in it and carrying it on, i.e., that the community exercises control over the conduct of its individual members; for it is this form that the social process or community enters as a determining factor into the individual's thinking" (p. 155).

Where does culture come in? From the symbolic interactionist point of view, the human individual—the self—is wide open to influence. As we have seen in our earlier discussion of meaning, biology or our innate nature gives little direction to our lives, so we have to develop our own guidelines, and we do so in the course of our interactions with one another. Symbolic interactionism suggests that human interactions create culture, just as Durkheim's corroboree created totemic religion. Once created, cultural objects are perpetuated and transmitted through their repeated expression and through the socialization of new group members—for example, the young. Symbolic interactionists are interested in the micro-settings through which this process happens.

Consider a classic interactionist paper by Howard Becker (1953) on how people learn to smoke marijuana. Many people think that getting high on marijuana is simply a biological response; the smoke from the cannabis leaves just "makes" the smoker high. On the contrary, Becker argued, a complex process of social learning must take place for someone to learn how to respond to marijuana. The novice smoker interacts with more experienced users, often with members of a marijuana subculture (at the time of the study, the early 1950s, marijuana smoking was primarily confined to jazz musicians and similar bohemian subcultures). From these experienced smokers, novices learn how to smoke (e.g., to hold the smoke in their lungs), what to feel (feelings such as floating or time distortion are identified and labeled by the experienced smokers), and what to enjoy. If the interaction process breaks down—for example, if a new user were trying to smoke a joint while all alone—the novice would be unlikely to develop the habit of or the taste for marijuana. But when all of the interaction processes are completed, the novice will have been socialized into marijuana smoking and might well go on to identify with the smokers' subculture. In the words of Becker's title, the smoker "becomes" a marijuana user, and smoking becomes part of his or her identity.

Similarly, one "becomes" a blues singer through interactions, not just through inborn talent. Bessie Smith's immediate musical heritage was not call-and-response work songs in the cotton fields—where the blues were

born—but the vaudeville stage and tent show circuit played by black performers in the early twentieth century. On the vaudeville circuit, women
singers developed a smooth, sophisticated style of singing, a far cry from
the earthy blues style of the fields. Indeed, it might be said that Smith's
innovation was not to sophisticate a folk idiom, but instead to rough up
this slick, cabaret singing. And even that wasn't strictly her own innovation. An immediate predecessor of Smith's, Ma (Gertrude) Rainey, traveled with touring companies throughout the South introducing down-
home elements into the vaudeville style. Rainey discovered Smith and
took her into her company, the Rabbit Foot Minstrels, where the young
girl's singing and showmanship developed. After leaving Rainey's troupe,
Smith worked the Southern circuit with tent shows, pursuing her career
in the world of segregated music. Bessie Smith's identity as a blues singer,
in other words, grew out of her interactions with other musicians.

Identity is a key concept for the symbolic interactionist approach.
One's own identity or sense of self—"I am a blues singer" or "I am a
brother-in-law"—is produced through interaction with others and requires
confirmation from others. Once again, we are in the realm of meanings
here; the self tries to project a certain set of meanings onto those with whom
it interacts, and in return tries to interpret the meanings constructed by
partners in the interaction. Erving Goffman (1959) analyzed this process
by using the metaphors of theatrical performances: When it interacts, the
self is an actor performing a role before an audience. If the performance
is successful, the self has confirmed a certain identity both to her partners
in interaction and to herself.

A striking example comes from research on the homeless. In their
study of homeless street people in a Texas city, David Snow and Leon
Anderson (1993) found that the down-and-out constantly try to do what
Snow and Anderson call "identity work": They manage their interactions
in such a way as to foster a specific set of impressions. Some construct
their identities in terms of distancing; they stress that they are "not like
the other guys who hang out down at the Sally" (p. 215) and therefore
don't need the services of the Salvation Army or other relief agencies.
Others embrace the homeless role—"I'm a bum, and I know who my friends
are" (p. 221)—declaring themselves to be proud of their freedom and clever
at surviving in the harsh world they inhabit. Still others construct elaborate fantasies about their past histories or future prospects. One homeless
man told the researchers at great length how the next day, "I'm going to
catch a plane to Pittsburgh and tomorrow night I'll take a hot bath, have
a dinner of linguine and red wine in my own restaurant, and have a woman
hanging on my arm" (p. 226). In all of these activities, the homeless are

conducting impression management in their interactions to control the meanings they present to others.

Again we see the cultural position as distinct from the biological one. A biologically based argument that Snow and Anderson cite (Maslow, 1962) suggests that human beings have a hierarchy of needs; they require certain things to survive—food, clothing, shelter—and only once these needs have been met do people have the luxury of worrying about meanings, identities, or symbolic representations. On the contrary, respond Snow and Anderson, the homeless, who may not know where their next meal is coming from or where they will sleep that night, are nevertheless adept manipulators of words and symbols, compelled to construct and project specific identities. Like all people, they use culture—in this case the resources of language and storytelling—to enact their social performances and make their world meaningful to themselves and to others.

Although the homeless have to make up their own culture and identities with few resources and limited precedents, most interactions that transmit culture and form identity call on a known and shared history of the community. The generalized other is usually concrete, with specific characteristics, in more stable social worlds, so the cultural objects that serve as collective representations do not have to be made up on the spot. Among the Yoruba in Nigeria, children are taught to greet their parents by kneeling in front of them before speaking. This kneeling is a form of etiquette, and the practice constitutes a meaningful cultural object. Through socialization into this practice, the child learns something about Yoruba relationships (the child must respect the adult) and behavior (the child must show respect in a particular way). The child also learns her collective identity. She is a Yoruba because she thinks and acts this way, and she thinks and acts this way because she is Yoruba.

Subcultures

To speak of Yoruba culture or identity is to evoke the image of an undifferentiated generalized other, a community to which all Yoruba belong. People, however, are members not simply of a single group or community, but of a variety of them. Mead (1934) identified two types: abstract social groups, such as debtors, that function as social groups only indirectly; and "concrete social classes or subgroups, such as political parties, clubs, corporations, which are all actually functioning social units, in terms of which of their individual members are directly related to one another" (p. 157). If these relations to one another are strong enough to counteract some of the influences of the societal generalized other, the group becomes a subculture.

The worlds of marijuana smokers, homeless men, or traveling vaudeville performers might well be referred to as *subcultures*. As the name suggests, a subculture exists within a larger cultural system and has contact with the external culture. Within the subculture's domain, however, operates a powerful set of symbols, meanings, and behavioral norms—often the opposite of those in the larger culture—that are binding on the subculture's members. Thus, we might speak of the youth gang subculture, the gay subculture, or the cyberpunk subculture. A subculture refers not only to consumption tastes—we don't speak of the subculture of Volvo owners or pizza lovers—but also to a way of life.

Subcultures, with their elaborate symbols and meanings, are produced by people interacting with one another and therefore have been of great interest to sociologists oriented toward symbolic interactionism. Gary Alan Fine (1987), for example, studied how members of Little League baseball teams produce their own temporary subcultures. Drawing on extensive participant observation, interviews, and questionnaires with ten Little League teams in three cities, Fine explored how social interaction in the Little League context (1) socializes boys into adult male roles and (2) gives rise to what Fine calls the "idioculture or self-culture" of the group.

To take an example of the socialization process, adults (coaches, parents) emphasize effort. They exhort the team to try harder by maintaining that a boy or a team has to "want to win" and that a player must always "give it his best shot." The unspoken assumption is that success or failure is dependent on internal motivation—on character, in other words—and not on physical talent, compatibility among team members' skills, or luck. The boys themselves emphasize "proper behavior," which they regard as the expression of appropriate emotions and emotional control. Both the adults and the boys themselves, therefore, socialize team members into a particular set of beliefs about masculine behavior and personality. These beliefs help shape appropriate behavior and attitudes for American adult males, including the conviction that success is a matter of individual responsibility and is not due to fate, external help, arbitrarily distributed skills, or physical resources. Moreover, big boys don't cry. In this way, culture constructions of gender are passed to a new generation. Socialization within this subculture does not subvert, but rather enacts, the socialization of the culture at large.

Fine's discussion of idioculture is concerned less with social psychology and more with the origins and determinants of cultural objects, such

Figure 3-1

Cultural Production in a Little League Baseball Team

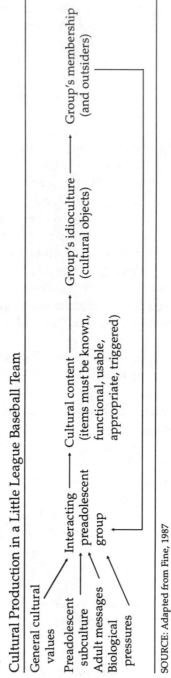

SOURCE: Adapted from Fine, 1987

58

as expressions and shared symbols. Little League teams develop an elaborate linguistic and symbolic code known only to the team members. One team, for example, designated a foul ball hit over the backstop as a "Polish home run." An outsider hearing jokes such as "Don't hit a Polish home run" might guess, based on his or her knowledge of American ethnic jokes about Poles, that the team referred to some inept play, but would have no idea of the specific act being referred to. Little League teams generate hundreds of such private, shared meanings.

Idioculture, therefore, is the culture of the subgroup: rich with implications, alive with symbols and expressions known only to insiders, and used to separate insiders from outsiders. The remarkable thing about a Little League team's idioculture is that, elaborate as it may be, it is constructed quickly and lasts a relatively short period of time, only as long as a baseball season. What are the roots of this idioculture? Fine's causal argument is sketched in Figure 3-1. The interacting preadolescent group—the team—responds to general cultural values, such as the importance of winning. The boys also participate in a preadolescent cultural system familiar to youths from coast to coast; what ten-year-old hasn't sung "A Hundred Bottles of Beer on the Wall"? Some of the cultural objects in this system come from the media, some from such institutions as summer camps where boys from different communities come together and trade information. The boys pick up messages from adults that are both direct and indirect, and they feel the influence of biological pressures, including an acute discomfort around girls. The most notable characteristic of this peer culture is a desperate longing to fit in with the other boys, coupled with a scorn for outsiders.

In such a context, events are transformed into culture. A boy was nicknamed "Maniac" because of his last name until his accuracy in fielding prompted his team to start calling him "Main Eye" instead. The coach's rusty old clunker was almost hit with a ball. "Don't dent my Cadillac," he joked, and for the rest of the season the team referred to the coach's Cadillac. Not just any event or object can undergo transformation into a cultural object, however. For a symbol or expression to enter the idioculture, it must draw on known information (e.g., ethnic slurs about Poles); it must be functional (nicknames help identify players, some of whom might have the same first name); it must be usable (certain four-letter words, well known in preadolescent subculture, are forbidden by coaches, so they do not enter most teams' idiocultures); it must be appropriate ("Maniac" stopped being an appropriate label for the cool and competent player); and it must be triggered repeatedly (the expression "Polish home run" would have been forgotten had not so many foul balls gone over the backstop).

Up to this point, we have considered the specific social world in which interactions take place, such as a subculture, as a relatively stable collectivity into which people are smoothly socialized. This is an incomplete view. In reality, societies change, culture changes, and changes in one realm influence changes in the other. To complete our understanding of culture as a social creation, we need to add this dynamic element into our model.

Cultural Innovation and Social Change

I have described how subcultures may perpetuate mainstream culture (the Little League teams) or defy it (the marijuana smokers), but sometimes they set out to change it. Although this is a relatively rare event— most subcultures just want to be left alone—many social movements start out as subcultures. To use Weber's terms, they move from the separation of other-worldly asceticism to the reforming or even revolutionary engagement of inner-worldly asceticism.

China offers a good example of how a separatist subculture became a movement for revolutionary social change. What became known as the Boxer Uprising of 1900 began as the Spirit Boxers, a subculture of peasant youth during the late Qing dynasty who were devoted to martial arts and a ritual involving the divine possession of a believer by one of the popular gods (Esherick, 1987). In 1898, the terrible poverty and dislocation brought about by the flooding of the Yellow River combined with increasing anti-Westernism in response to escalating imperialist and missionary activities to transform the Boxers into a militant nationalist movement, the Boxers United in Righteousness. Their slogan was "Revive the Qing, destroy the foreign." Over the next two years, the numbers of Boxers grew, as did their attacks on Chinese Christians and the foreigners themselves, finally culminating in a siege of the foreign enclave in Beijing that was put down by a foreign expeditionary force amid great bloodshed.

Although secret societies or spirit possession cults were not unusual in the late Qing, specific social pressures—increasing foreign demands and routine poverty exacerbated by natural disaster—turned what had been an "other-worldly" subculture into a movement bent on radical social transformation. The very meaning of the Boxers' cultural objects changed. Martial arts, for example, initially had represented individual discipline and self-control to the Spirit Boxers. To the Boxers United in Righteousness, it meant aggressive Chinese nationalism. How would we describe this in terms of the cultural diamond? Did a change in the social world (increasing foreign pressures) produce a change in the cultural object (martial arts)? Or did the development of a cultural object (the increasing popularity of martial arts among youth) produce a change in the way the young Chinese viewed the social world? We need to take a closer look now at the relationship between cultural innovations and societal changes.

Cultural Lags and Leads

Reflection theories of either the Marxist or the functionalist stamp, as was discussed previously, could not answer these questions very well. If culture passively reflects the social world, which is what the reflection model usually implies, then change must come from that world first. In this view, innovations in music, art, theology, ideas, popular culture, literature, and expressive behavior must all be responses to social changes. Now although there is clearly something right about the idea that social shifts produce cultural changes, such a deterministic position suggests that the social world always changes first, with culture lagging behind.

The "cultural lag" hypothesis was put forward by a sociologist named William Ogburn ([1922] 1936), who maintained that sociologists should distinguish between "material culture" and "adaptive culture." Material culture is just what it sounds like: "home, factories, machines, raw materials, manufactured products, food stuffs and other material objects." When this material culture changes, the nonmaterial culture, which includes practices, folkways, and social institutions, must change in response. Adaptive culture is the portion of nonmaterial culture that adjusts to material conditions. It always takes a while for the adaptations to catch up with material changes, and this gap is the "cultural lag." Ogburn used the example of the American forests. At one time, the material conditions (vast forests) were matched by social practices (large-scale timbering, clearing forests for agriculture). The destruction of the forests constituted a dramatic change in American material culture, but it was many years before serious efforts at conservation and reforestation were made at the level of adaptive culture—hence the cultural lag.

Ogburn believed that changes in the material culture usually precede changes in the adaptive culture. In some sense, this is true by definition (adaptation means adapting *to* something). Such a theory is compatible with reflection theory in both its functionalist and Marxian forms. At the same time, we can easily come up with examples wherein nonmaterial culture leads, not lags behind, material conditions. Max Weber's account of how the spirit of capitalism burned hot in backwoods eighteenth-century Pennsylvania is one such example. For another, consider the worldwide changes in cigarette smoking. Neither a material change (there was no scarcity of tobacco) nor a material discovery (the dangers of smoking to health had been known for years) prompted the abrupt decline of smoking among the American and (later) the European middle classes. The change in attitude came when the large generation born after World War II became concerned (some might say obsessed) with health and fitness. For baby boomers, the body—exercised, slimmed, well cared for—represented an ideal of youth and strength. High status was demonstrated not with martinis, fur coats, and silver cigarette cases, but with expensive mineral water, jogging, and disdain for smokers. As a cultural object for this group, the cigarette came to mean a foolish, and irritating to others, disregard for bodily health. As rates of smoking plummeted, tobacco companies had to adjust their material culture by manufacturing "slim" and "low tar" cigarettes and by aggressively marketing their products in Africa and Asia to make up for the loss of American and European smokers. To a large extent, cigarettes have now become a Third World cultural object.

The idea that culture always lags behind material change also goes against our experience with dramatic cultural change. As the humanities have long emphasized, now and then a genius, a prophet, an innovator bursts on the scene and shakes up existing cultural conventions. At a collective level, some new cultural movements—abstract expressionism, punk music, New Age spirituality, the African American women novelists of the 1970s, prime-time serials, or the rage for physical fitness—emerge and prosper without any direct push from the social. So we need to understand this cultural innovation, where culture seems to lead, not lag behind, social change, or where cultural change seems to bear no direct relation to changes happening in the society at large.

Cultural Innovations

A random event—a boy hits a ball over the backstop, to the chagrin of his teammates—gets processed by group interaction. The symbolic representation of the event is functional, in that it is useful for building group solidarity, identifying norms, and separating the insiders from the outsiders. Cultural creation has occurred, and a cultural innovation—the "Polish home run"—gets established. More generally, the collective production approach to culture suggests that, although innovations may occur randomly and unpredictably, some patterns are evident: (1) Certain periods are more likely to generate innovations than others, (2) even the innovations follow some conventions, and (3) certain innovations are more likely than others to become established.

Let's look at these points in order. A number of cultural analysts have argued that cultural creativity does not take place at a steady rate, but shows dramatic peaks and valleys. There are periods of relatively little change, during which conventions are stable, ideas are generally shared by the community in question, and the status quo is unchallenged—individual selves and the generalized others are in harmony, Mead might say. At other times, cultural creativity explodes. Thinkers come up with new ideas and systems of ideas, and these are circulated among men and women concerned about public affairs. Artists defy the conventions of their genres. Long-standing relations, such as those between the sexes, get overturned. Behaviors change in everything from dress to living arrangements to occupational goals. In much of the world, the 1960s represented such a period of intense cultural ferment.

What causes such a burst of cultural innovation? "Unsettled times," says sociologist Ann Swidler (1986). A "disturbance in the moral order," says Robert Wuthnow (1987). A loosening up of the dominant ideology, says Marxian critic Raymond Williams ([1973] 1980). The common point they are making seems to be that under certain conditions—massive demographic shift, war, sudden economic change—the old rules, cultural and social, no longer seem to apply. A moral vacuum occurs, and in such a situation people cast around for new guidelines, new meanings with which to orient their lives. Failure to find such meanings brings the experience of anomie, the disorientation that Durkheim attributed to rapid social change. Cultural innovation—the production of new meanings—emerges as a response to incipient anomie. It reorients people and gives them their bearings in the new social circumstances.

Think again of the middle and late 1960s. The United States experienced a controversial war; unusual but unevenly distributed economic prosperity; legislation bringing the agenda of African Americans, other minorities, and (later) women into mainstream politics; and a demographic bulge (the baby boom) that was going through its teenage years. This combination lay the ground for extraordinary cultural change. Ideologies, fads, artistic movements, behavioral changes—from cohabitation to long hair to the drug culture to Pop Art to the Black Panthers to Women's Liberation to acid rock—all represented cultural responses to the unsettled times that were the 1960s. (In many respects, the slower pace of cultural change from the mid-1970s until the present may be seen as a consolidation of the changes made during the previous decade.)

The innovations of the 1960s were not just an American phenomenon. The withdrawal of colonialism from Nigeria, as elsewhere in Africa, stimulated a burst of artistic and intellectual activity. In contrast, the failure of such economic programs as the Great Leap Forward and Mao's increasing uneasiness over the future of the Chinese Communist regime lay the groundwork for the Cultural Revolution, clearly an innovation in the extent and ferocity of its repression. In Europe, youth culture, spurred by the baby boom, consumerism, and left-wing politics, shook the traditional establishment.

Does all of this mean that cultural lag theorists were right—that culture changes in response to the social world? Although the arguments of Wuthnow and Swidler may seem to suggest this, the issue of what leads what depends largely on when you start the analysis. We could say that the ongoing Chinese Communist revolution (social world, material culture) led to the Cultural Revolution (cultural objects, adaptive culture). But we could just as legitimately say, rather, that earlier changes in the Chinese culture (modernization, the impact of the West) led to changes in the Chinese social world (the Communist Revolution).

By the 1980s—to take another example of the ambiguity of leads and lags—there was general agreement in the U.S. on the belief that women deserved equal pay for equal work. Furthermore, the popular media were filled with images of strong, highly successful women, such as the television heroines who managed high-powered careers, multiple adorable children, and passionate love lives while looking gorgeous all the time. Advertisers appealed to the briefcase-carrying careerist who had "come a long way, baby." But this shared image of the affluent career woman was not matched by reality, wherein women continued to earn far less than their male counterparts. In this case, the culture seems to "lead" the economic reality (or, in Marxian terms, superstructure was leading the base). The issue of leads and lags is less important than the fact that a cultural shift regarding women (including mothers) clearly had taken place, starting in the 1960s, and institutions—from pay scales to day care to sharing of housework in the home—were and are slow to catch up.

Although certain periods seem to exhibit more cultural change than others, the second premise of the collective production approach to innovation is that cultural innovations may not be as dramatically different as they first seem. Cultural creators typically respond to conventions, rather than ignore them. Howard Becker (1982), for example, distinguished four types of artists: the integrated professionals, the mavericks, the naive artists, and the folk artists. Three of the four types are conventional. Folk artists follow the conventions of their craft. Integrated professionals perpetuate the conventions of their own particular art world (Becker uses the term art world to encompass all of the people whose various activities —from making paintbrushes, for example, to writing art criticism—go into the production of a certain kind of art). Mavericks ostentatiously defy the art world's conventions, but the key point is that their very unconventionality can be recognized only by those who know the conventions in the first place. They are being conventionally unconventional, like teenagers who express their nonconformity with adult values by conforming to a rigid teenage dress code designed to appall their elders. Only naive artists, who are not attached to a collective production world, may be said to innovate without regard for convention, but their very lack of connections makes the work of such artists virtually unknown. Thus, their innovations have neither audience nor influence.

Which brings us to the third premise on innovation: Cultural creators may produce something new, but not all such innovations will become established. We saw this in Fine's Little League study; a new symbol or ickname will wither unless conditions allow it to become known, used, functional, apt, and repeatedly triggered. On a larger scale, Robert Wuthnow (1985) suggested that ideological innovations of the modern era are unlikely to last unless the state is hospitable to them. Looking at the Reformation in Europe, he pointed out that monarchs were always favorable to some version of Luther's reforms, for the Reformation downgraded ecclesiastical authority and thus removed Rome and the church hierarchy as a major rival to royal authority. Whether or not the Reformation took hold in a particular country, therefore, was a consequence of how powerful the king or queen was in comparison to the landed aristocracy, which favored Rome. Countries with a relatively strong monarchy, such as England, embraced the Reformation, whereas countries with a monarchy dependent on the landed aristocracy, such as France, did not.

Similarly, Bessie Smith's singing was innovative, but that's not the only reason it was so successful. It caught on, became established, only because of a specific set of conditions. Her timing was lucky: In 1920, a singer named Mamie Smith (no relation) made the first blues record, "Crazy Blues," and opened up a vast new market for the record industry. Within a few years, Okey, Paramount, and Columbia's "Race Record" series were seeking singers for the African-American market. Bessie Smith was signed up by Columbia, and her recordings for them were the basis of her immense popularity. She continued to tour the vaudeville circuit in the South, but the Columbia recordings had created an audience in the North as well. She played in large Northern cities under the auspices of the Theatre Owners Booking Association. (T.O.B.A. was considered to be the best management and booking agent for Negro performers, but its demands gave it the nickname among the stars of "Tough On Black Asses.") Indeed, much of Smith's reputation for innovation is due to her introducing a Southern musical form to a Northern audience.

Bessie Smith's story is unquestionably one of individual talent, but it is also one of record companies and vaudeville circuits, artistic mentors and new audiences, expanding markets and skilled promotion. Her blues were both a collective representation of African American life in the segregated South and a collective product of an entertainment industry. Although her genius was her own, her creation was social.

Summary

In this chapter, we have traced some sociological theories of the creation of culture. We have seen how sociologists have followed Durkheim in regarding culture as collective product or representation, rather than as exclusively the work of individual creators. Cultural objects, by this reasoning, express aspects of the social world and are produced by the collective activities of members of this world. We have seen how interactions among people create new cultural objects—practices, beliefs, symbols, expressions—and how such cultural objects bestow meanings on the human experience. We have seen how cultural innovation, creating new meaning, occurs at the micro level of subcultures and the macro level of ideological shifts. We have seen that creativity, along with its recognition and its establishment, depends on social conventions and social institutions.

Figure 3-2 offers a visual summary of our increasingly complex, and increasingly sociological, understanding of cultural creation. Diagram (1) is the genius view: An extraordinary individual creates an new cultural object. Diagram (2) is a straight reflection argument: The individual drops out, and the cultural object is a pure collective representation. In diagram (3) the cultural creator is influenced by the larger social world in which she is located; she is part of an interacting community and its conventions. Both the social world and the interacting community (which may be a subculture) influence her creation. And the success of this creator's innovation involves another collective process, one that determines whether or not the cultural object reaches its potential recipients.

So far, we have concentrated on creators of culture on one hand and the social world on the other. We have paid only minimal attention to two things: the audience or recipients of culture (the right point on our culture diamond), and the organizations of production and distribution that tie

Figure 3-2

Cultural Creation

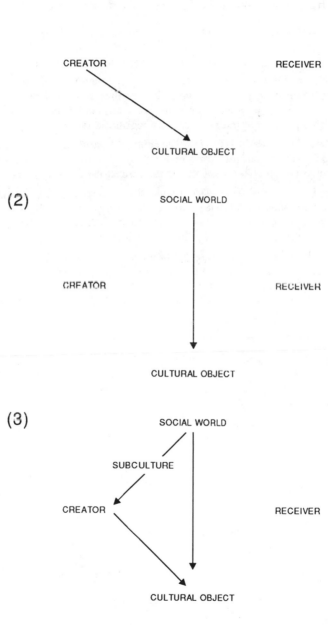

all of the points together. Yet we have seen in the example of Bessie Smith that organizations and audiences are vital to any understanding of cultural creations as collective representation. These two—the right point of our cultural diamond and the organization as links among creators, receivers, and cultural objects—are the subject of the next chapter.

RECOMMENDED FOR FURTHER READING

Becker, Howard S. 1982. *Art Worlds.* Berkeley: University of California Press. A lively account of how a wide variety of human activities and interactions produce art and how whether or not a cultural object gets the label of "art" is itself a product of interactions and negotiations.

Durkheim, Emile. (1915) 1965. *The Elementary Forms of the Religious Life.* Joseph Ward Swain, trans. New York: Free Press. No summary can capture the rich detail of Durkheim's study or the precision of his analysis.

Goffman, Erving. 1959. *The Presentation of Self in Everyday Life.* Garden City, NY: Doubleday. The classic sociological interpretation of the idea that "all the world's a stage," Goffman's dramaturgical analysis of everyday life has been immensely influential to later sociologists.

Wuthnow, Robert. 1987. *Meaning and Moral Order: Explorations in Cultural Analysis.* Berkeley: University of California Press. A serious effort to come to grips with cultural innovation. Wuthnow differs from the approach suggested in this book in his argument that cultural sociology should move "beyond meaning."

4

The Production, Distribution, and Reception of Culture

Many Americans and Canadians proudly display Eskimo soapstone carvings in their living rooms.[1] Rounded, polished, smooth to the touch, these miniature sculptures of polar bears, seals, and fur-wrapped children adorn any number of urban middle-class homes thousands of miles from the Arctic. The carvings seem profoundly natural, the innocent, simple renditions of what the Eskimos see around them. By now, of course, readers of this book will have learned to be wary when anything is referred to as "natural." The sociological approach to culture maintains that practices or objects that seem natural, even inevitable, are not. Like Marx's cherry tree, they have a history embedded in social relations. As do the soapstone carvings.

According to anthropologist Nelson Grayburn (1967), military men stationed in the far north during World War II and other visitors noticed the Eskimo penchant for carving or whittling. The Eskimos looked on this activity as making toys, not art, doing something to amuse the children and pass the time during the dark months of an Arctic winter. An entrepreneurial Canadian artist named James Houston saw something else in these little carvings—namely, the appeal they would have for non-Eskimo viewers and buyers in the cities to the south. With the encouragement of the Canadian Department of Northern Affairs, which was responsible for the Eskimos' welfare, Houston set up a system of production for the market he had so astutely identified.

At first there were problems. Because the Eskimos worked with extremely hard materials such as ivory and bone, carving took a long time. Ivory, moreover, was increasingly rare. These things hardly mattered when

---

[1]Most native North Americans of the Arctic, who used to be called Eskimos, now prefer to call themselves and be called Inuit. I follow Grayburn (1967), who used the term *Eskimo* in his research; the soapstone sculptures under discussion here are commonly referred to as *Eskimo art*.

the carvers were producing for their own amusement, but the organizers from down south and their marketing outlets in lower Canada and the United States were spiritual heirs of Benjamin Franklin—"Time is money" —and the leisurely rhythms and small quantities of craft production did not fit their requirements. They convinced the Eskimos to work in soapstone, which was both readily available and easy to carve, so they could turn out the finished carvings more quickly.

The content as well as the materials of these carvings required some regulation. When Eskimo inmates in a tuberculosis hospital decided to make some money with their carving, they turned out sculptures of American cars and kangaroos. Another course correction was needed. The entrepreneurs destroyed these carvings and impressed on the carvers that the customers in Toronto and New York seeking "real" Eskimo art wanted seals and bears, not kangaroos. No doubt bemused by what the white people in warm climates found interesting, the Eskimos dutifully turned out the roly-poly animals as required. Carvers in another Eskimo community were encouraged to fashion figures from their traditional religious mythology, and they happily obliged even though they had been devout Anglicans for generations.

Just as the entrepreneur had envisioned, the carvings caught on and found their market. A system of production and distribution was set up that remains today. The Eskimos got a new source of income, the gallery owners in Canadian and American cities got their percentage, the entrepreneurs made money, and coffee tables from Winnipeg to Atlanta displayed fat little seals that their owners assumed and still assume to be traditional folk art.

This story about culture demonstrates what we have previously suggested: Cultural objects such as the soapstone carvings are not simply the "natural" products of some social context; instead, they are produced, distributed, marketed, received, and interpreted by a variety of people and organizations. This kind of self-conscious production, marketing, and distribution system applies to ideas as much as it does to tangible cultural objects. During the years leading up to the Iranian revolution, the Ayatollah Khomeini taped speeches propounding his brand of fundamentalist Islam during his exile in Paris. His followers smuggled the tapes into Iran, and the faithful secretly listened to them on cassette players. International broadcasters such as CNN similarly package ideas and frame news events and then distribute them throughout the world. And it is now possible to send prayers and petitions to Jerusalem's Wailing Wall by fax.

In this chapter we explore the production, distribution, and reception of culture. We have already glimpsed some of these processes—recall Bessie Smith with her "Race Records," touring companies, and newly created Northern audiences—and now we take a closer look at the organizations and processes whereby cultural objects move beyond their creators to those who ultimately experience, consume, and interpret them. We start with the production-of-culture school of cultural analysis. Next follows a discussion of audiences and cultural reception in which we consider the implications of the fact that the receivers of a cultural object come to it not as blank slates, but as people conditioned by their cultural and social experiences. Finally, we look at two opposing interpretations of the production-reception link: the pessimistic view of the "mass culture" theorists and the more optimistic view held by scholars of "popular culture."

The Production of Culture

Many sociologists have believed that it is insufficient simply to point out, following Durkheim or Marx, that culture is a collective product. We need to understand just how culture—and the cultural objects that compose a culture—is produced; moreover, we need to learn what impact the means and processes of production have on cultural objects themselves. This type of analysis came out of industrial and organizational sociology during the early 1970s, when sociologists trained in industrial sociology, systems analysis, and economic analyses of business firms began applying their models to cultural production.

This new production-of-culture approach, in the words of Richard Peterson (one of its founders and foremost practitioners), looks at the "complex apparatus which is interposed between cultural creators and consumers" (Peterson, 1978, p. 295; see also Peterson, 1976). This apparatus includes facilities for production and distribution; marketing techniques such as advertising, co-opting mass media, or targeting; and the creation of situations that bring potential cultural consumers in contact with cultural objects. Placing racks of paperbacks in a supermarket, signing a new singer with a record company, legwork done before and after a Billy Graham rally, organizing a blockbuster museum exhibit, getting publicity for a new trend in fashion—all of these activities are grist for the production-of-culture mill.

The Culture Industry System

We can begin thinking about cultural production by working from a framework developed for mass-produced cultural objects. Paul Hirsch (1972) developed a useful model that he calls the "culture industry system"—in other words, the organizations that produce mass culture staples such as records, popular books, and low-budget films. Hirsch pointed out that such cultural objects share a number of features. First is demand uncertainty; no one knows what the market will be for a new film, for example. Second is a relatively cheap technology, and third is an oversupply of would-be cultural creators—all of those singers, filmmakers, and authors clutching their manuscripts. In the light of these factors, the culture industry system works to regulate and package innovation and thus to transform creativity into predictable, marketable packages. Figure 4.1 shows how Hirsch's system works.

Starting at the left of Figure 4-1, we see the creators (the artists, the geniuses, the talent) transformed into the technical subsystem. This is an extreme statement of the collective production viewpoint, which regards individuals with various degrees of creative skill and inspiration as a subsystem that provides "input" for the rest of the system. This input must cross the boundary at Filter #1. Recall that there is an oversupply in the technical subsystem; it contains many more would-be artists (singers, filmmakers, novelists) than the overall system requires. At the input boundary, the creative artists employ "boundary spanners," such as agents, to bring their work to the attention of the producing organization. Or they may act as their own agents; an aspiring author of a romance novel, for example, will send a query to a romance publisher, describing the novel she (usually) wants to write and asking whether the publisher might be interested. The producing organization employs its own boundary spanners—talent scouts who check out new bands, editors who read through piles of manuscripts, directors who look for promising screenplays.

The managerial subsystem consists of the organizations that actually produce the product: publishing houses, film studios, record companies. Sometimes these are large firms, but sometimes they are not. For example, publishing is a business in which virtually everything can be subcontracted out, so a "publishing house" might consist of a single individual with a telephone. Sometimes it is not even that. In Nigeria, authors can arrange to have their books typeset and run off by the local newspaper printer; the name of a fictitious "publisher" then appears on the book even though no such organizational entity exists. Another twist to the managerial subsystem is that, although Hirsch was thinking of culture-producing

Figure 4-1

The Culture Industry System

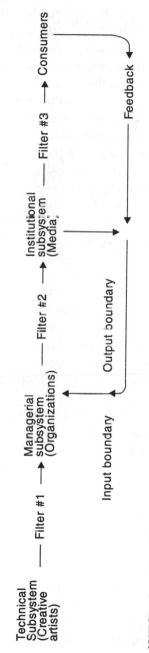

SOURCE: Adapted from Hirsch (1972)

organizations turning out a large number of similar products, in some cases an organization exists only to produce a single cultural object. This is cal project-based organization and is characteristic, for example, of independent filmmaking wherein contracts tie the director, producer, and actors together only for the duration of the project (Faulkner & Anderson, 1987).

Strategies that the managerial subsystem employs to manage innovation include maintaining contact personnel at both boundaries, overproduction of products coupled with the recognition that most will fail, and unremitting attempts to influence or co-opt media gatekeepers. At the output boundary, the producing organization employs boundary spanners to reach the mass media—the crucial target of promotional activities—with news about the "product" (Filter #2). Media gatekeepers (the institutional subsystem) include such people as disc jockeys, talk show hosts, book and film reviewers, and that portion of the press that covers culture and its creators. For large firms, publicity and sales departments cultivate relations with the media, who serve as surrogate consumers. There is plenty of room for corruption here, as in the occasional payola scandals wherein record companies bribe disc jockeys to promote their latest records.

The ultimate consumers—the public—typically hear of new products through the media (Filter #3). If Siskel and Ebert give a film two thumbs up, their television viewers will be more inclined to see it. Although the producing organizations are highly dependent on such media exposure and work hard to get it, they also work hard to avoid needing it. This is done either by producing a fairly homogeneous product or by convincing consumers that you have done so. An example of the first strategy would be the various lines of romance novels. Readers know precisely what a Harlequin romance will be like; they know the basic plot formulas, they know the degree of sexual explicitness, they know the length. That being the case, Harlequin does not need to advertise or promote each individual new novel. Instead, it promotes the lines—Harlequin Romance, Harlequin American Romance, Harlequin Suspense—and emphasizes the homogeneity of the lines by giving each new title a number. The second strategy is to indicate more product homogeneity than actually exists. Promoting the "new Woody Allen film" or the "latest album by Prince" is a way of trying to bypass the media (who may say, after all, that this latest album by Prince is not as good as his earlier ones) by convincing consumers that if they liked earlier work by a certain singer or director, they are sure to like the new product.

Two types of feedback take place in the culture industry system. The first comes from the media and consists of air time, reviews, and general media attention. The second comes from consumers and is measured by sales of tickets, records, or books; by jukebox plays; and by sales of related products (a hit movie such as *Beauty and the Beast* is surrounded by an enormous cloud of products, from books to lunch boxes to stuffed animals to, finally, the movie video itself). Producing organizations interpret both types of feedback to assess the popularity of an artist, the effectiveness of their promotional activities, and implications for similar future productions.

Notice that we can superimpose Hirsch's model on the horizontal axis of the cultural diamond. Doing so emphasizes what should already be clear: The actual cultural object, the product of the managerial subsystem, is of minor importance in the total system. This is especially true for the mass culture products Hirsch had in mind, which are overproduced; the producing organization has no great stake in any one product so long as a certain percentage of its products are hits.

Hirsch developed his culture industry model specifically for tangible mass culture products, but with minimal modification it could be applied to high culture, ideas, or any other cultural object. If, for example, we were to take a certain theological stance (let's say a feminist reading of the Bible) as our cultural object, we can think of a religious denomination in analogous terms to a culture industry system, turning out theological messages as its products or, in other words, as cultural objects. The technical subsystem consists of seminary graduates looking for positions. The managerial subsystem is the churches of the denomination (for simplicity, we can assume a congregational polity like the Baptists, in which individual churches select or "call" their own pastors). Newly ordained graduates ask boundary spanners such as mentors from the seminary to help them locate a position; meanwhile, churches have their own boundary spanners in the form of pastoral search committees out canvassing the "talent." A would-be pastor's feminism may be an asset or a liability for any given church, just as a recording artist's style may be attractive or unattractive to a record company's talent scouts. Once the pastor has attained a ministry—has been taken on by a culture-producing organization in the managerial subsystem—his message, via sermons, rituals, and setting a pastoral example, would go out to the consumers, the members of the congregation. An institutional subsystem such as the local press may feature the new pastor and his innovations; in rare cases, churches employ a more elaborate use of radio or television to broadcast sermons and services. The most important medium, however, is word-of-mouth. Feedback from the congregation comes directly to the pastor and to the lay leaders of the church. More dramatic feedback, analogous to ticket sales, comes from membership changes. If the pastor is popular, if his innovative combination of biblical literalism and feminism goes over well, word spreads in the community and the congregation grows. On the other hand, if he is at odds with his congregation, if the fit between his theology and their piety is a poor one, church members may vote with their feet and membership declines, prompting the church to go back to the technical subsystem in search of new talent.

The model of the culture industry system can be applied to cases from nonindustrial societies as well. In many West African societies, for example, young men want to join the secret societies that perform masquerades (in this system, the cultural object) on ritual occasions. Only a specific secret society is allowed to put on a specific masquerade. There is an oversupply of would-be masquerade dancers in the technical subsystem, and these young men may encourage kin and patrons to spread the word about their performing abilities. The secret society itself is equivalent to the managerial subsystem, and its members would scout for talent. (The roles of the boundary spanners are especially interesting in this case because no one actually knows or can admit knowing who the members of a secret society are, nor can the members reveal themselves.) The institutional subsystem operates via word of mouth; if a secret society is especially good at masquerading, people from neighboring villages may show up at the proper time to try to catch the performance. Negative feedback is also popular; a poor masquerade may be mocked by village youth, and the secret society may have to rework its performance accordingly.

By these examples, we can see that analytic models such as Hirsch's help us understand how culture-producing organizations work. Such organizations attempt to produce a regular flow of products and reduce uncertainty. But despite the controlling efforts of the managerial subsystem, a great deal of unpredictability does come from the market—those ticket buyers, congregants, audiences, consumers, potential converts who ultimately will determine the success of a cultural object. We need, therefore, to examine the nature of markets more closely.

Cultural Markets

Richard Peterson (1978) studied the production of cultural change in country music, and his research offers a good example of how market changes can reverberate throughout a culture industry system. Peterson described the production of country music. The culture industry system for this music (to use Hirsch's terms) was fairly small, generally rural and white, and had a high degree of integration among its subsystems. Record companies or their subunits were themselves devoted to country music. Singers traveled the performance circuit—including Nashville venues, state and county fairs, and country music festivals—and often sang live on country radio stations. Country stations, advertising such products as seed, fertilizer, and chewing tobacco, appealed to a rural audience. In this system, the artists and country disc jockeys often knew each other, and the deejays who played country music exclusively were very familiar with the music and its performers. There was, finally, a close fit in the lifestyles of performers and their audience.

Change came in the form of a hip-swinging white kid named Elvis Presley, who created a sensation in the mid-1950s by mixing the traditional country sound with black rhythm and blues. Feeling threatened by the explosive demand for rock and roll, and fearing that their own brand of music might get swamped, country singers banded together to form the Country Music Association, dedicated to the preservation and promotion of their musical style. The C.M.A. was extremely, and paradoxically, successful in its efforts. Peterson showed the dramatic increase in the number of country music stations that occurred during the 1960s and early 1970s. This increase brought with it some unexpected consequences. The new stations, now competing for a broader market, needed to extend their audience appeal beyond the traditional country music fans. So they began taking some of the hard edges off the country sound, playing songs that sounded less twangy and more like rock. These stations (the institutional subsystem) called themselves "modern country radio," and they began to resemble the "top 40" stations. Disc jockeys (gatekeepers at Filter #2) who served the new stations were no longer very knowledgeable about country music; they preferred, and played, the songs that sounded most like rock.

Some recording artists gained immense popularity due to the expansion of the country music sound, but many of the old troupers found themselves cut out of the "modern country" market as rock and easy-listening styles prevailed. Old singing styles such as cowboy music were squeezed out entirely. The record industry responded to the changing market in its choice of talent (Filter #1). More singers felt compelled to adopt a crossover strategy, singing country-rock blends. Traditionalists formed a new organization, the Association of Country Entertainers, to fight the dilution of the country sound, but with limited success. Record companies favored crossover sounds; modern country radio, eager to capture an ever wider audience and show advertisers they could reach affluent urban consumers (no more ads for chewing tobacco), emphasized familiar songs and recent hits. Country music became less and less distinguish-able from other popular music.

In this case, a large new market worked to diminish the artistic distinct-iveness of a cultural object, but the opposite can happen as well: Increased market size can result in cultural differentiation. Consider a case from a very different time and place, nineteenth-century Paris. Harrison and Cynthia White (1965) showed how the French dealer-critic system rose in the mid-nineteenth century to challenge the dominance of the Royal Academy and serve the growing bourgeoisie. The conservative Academy, with its annual juried Salons, favored huge paintings of classical, patri-otic, and religious subjects. Paintings of landscapes or humble subjects were rarely exhibited. But the growing market of middle-class house-holders did not want monumental depictions of "The death of Caesar" or "Jesus scourging the moneylenders" on their living room walls. They wanted what was pretty, familiar, a pleasure to the eye. At about the same time, technical changes in the manufacture of pigments made it possible for artists to leave the studios and paint in the open air. The new market organized by independent dealers coincided with the new technology, as well as with the needs of an increasing number of painters to have a steady income, something that the Academy Salons could provide only to a tiny minority. The cultural objects that resulted from this new combination of dealers, critics, buyers, and painters were fresh, vivid renditions of natu-ral scenes and middle-class life, with all of the brush strokes showing and nary a martyr or classical hero in view. In this manner, Impressionism, originally the work of a few Salon rejects, was established as one of the most important and popular innovations in the post-Renaissance visual arts.

A similar innovation-through-exclusion process took place with Ameri-can novels during the nineteenth century (Griswold, 1981). At this time, American copyright laws protected Americans but not foreigners, which meant that publishers had to pay royalties to native authors but not to English ones. As always there was an oversupply of manuscripts, and as always publishers wanted to maximize profit, so American publishers favored English novels. This preference led to a curious result. American writers who wrote about the same subjects that English writers wrote about—love and marriage, money and achievement, the joys and sorrows of middle-class social life—were blocked at Filter #1 because the pub-lisher could get that kind of novel from English authors without paying royalties. (The English authors made no profits on works published in the United States either, and they complained bitterly about the American "piracy.") Accordingly, those American novels that did get published tended to deal with unusual, non-middle-class subjects, often telling about men or boys who fled society and had adventures in the wilderness. Many of the classics of our literature—*Moby Dick, Huckleberry Finn, The Deerslayer* —follow this model. Critics ever since have speculated on the peculiarities in the American character or psychology that have produced so many "men outside society" novels and so few "love, money, and manners" novels. A production-of-culture analysis, however, suggests that such novels were the result of quirks in the American copyright law, not in the American character. When the United States finally adopted international copyright in 1891, most of the thematic differences between American and English novels simply disappeared.

Markets influence cultural production, but not always by excluding or driving out one type of cultural object in favor of another. Sometimes parallel markets can coexist with considerable stability. Liah Greenfeld (1989) mapped the "different worlds" of Israeli art, in which two systems of cultural production and consumption operate side by side in this tiny country with virtually no contact. The one system supports abstract art; its market consists of influential intellectuals and state bureaucrats who buy for museum collections. The other system supports representational art; it is supported by the business class and the galleries and dealers who sell to it. Each system has its own artists, market, audience, and styles, as well as its own system of critical evaluation. Members of each system, moreover, have a certain degree of contempt for members of the other.

No matter how stable a system may be, cultural markets respond to social change. As we saw in Chapter 3, it is probably pointless to debate what leads or lags behind what. There seem to be certain "unsettled" periods when both the social world, including its economic and political arrangements, and the expressive objects that we call culture change more rapidly than usual. Such times are fertile for the production of new ideologies and new genres, and under such circumstances cultural markets and cultural forms change together.

An example of dramatic social and cultural change producing a new cultural market and new cultural forms to satisfy this market comes from early twentieth-century China. During the late nineteenth century, China experienced severe political crises, including the Boxer Uprising discussed in Chapter 3, caused by the Qing dynasty's increasingly apparent incapacity to defend China against foreign incursions. Urban Chinese, especially those living in treaty ports with foreign enclaves and rapid industrialization such as Shanghai, had a growing appetite for news of all kinds, and the number of newspapers and presses grew dramatically (Lee & Nathan, 1985). With more and more Chinese becoming literate and demanding both news and new ways of thinking, some writers took upon themselves the obligation to instruct their fellow citizens about the changing world. Others, inspired by the growing urban market, simply wanted to entertain readers and make some money. And for many, the impulses toward entertainment and instruction were intertwined.

Beginning about 1910, "butterfly fiction," which depicted true love and ill-fated lovers, was immensely popular, especially in Shanghai (Link, 1981). These stories and novels were written by educated men whose employment prospects had been destroyed by the end of the civil service exam system in 1905. Drawn to Shanghai, they saw their chance with the booming readership, especially that huge urban middle class who wanted to read but didn't want anything too challenging. The butterfly love stories were non-Western and affirmed some traditional Chinese values, but at the same time they glorified true love and marital choice. This was happening at a time when, for many urban Chinese, family-arranged marriages were giving way to a freer choice of mates. Thus, butterfly fiction may be seen, after Durkheim, as a collective representation, reflecting and addressing new ways of thinking about love and marriage. But it was also a response to a distinctive urban context of literary production shaped by the migration of educated men (technical subsystem), a vigorous press (managerial subsystem), interacting circles of socially aware intellectuals (institutional subsystem), and an ever increasing market of literate Chinese.

But what part does the consumer play in this range of examples? In this discussion of the culture industry system, we have given short shrift to this vital element. (Hirsch didn't even regard consumers as a "system.") So far we have been concentrating on the connections among cultural creators, objects, and receivers—the lines (diamond-wise) among the three points captured by the "culture industry system" or the "market"—but we have not focused on the right point of the cultural diamond, the consumers, receivers, or audiences for cultural objects. It's time to do so. In the spirit of Hirsch's model, we might call cultural receivers the "interpretation-producing subsystem." In the next section we look at how receivers interpret cultural objects in order to produce their own meanings.

Reception

Despite all of the strategies employed by core firms in culture industry systems, a great deal of uncertainty remains. Record companies cannot predictably produce hit records anymore than publishers can reliably turn out best-sellers. Pastoral recruitment committees often find that their taste in ministers turns out to be at odds with the preferences of their congregations. Brilliant ideas fall on deaf ears. The ultimate success of a cultural object depends on its listeners or viewers, its audiences, its consumers—in other words, on the cultural recipients who make their own meanings from it. For although the meaning of a cultural object may be initially suggested by the intentions or period eye of its creators, the receivers of culture have the last word. We need to consider how and with what degree of freedom receivers make cultural objects meaningful.

Audiences and Taste Cultures

Survey research supports what common observation shows: Different types of people watch, buy, enjoy, use, read, and believe different cultural objects. Devotees of dogfights tend to be working class and male; devotees of opera tend to be upper class and white. Mainstream Protestants tend to be more affluent and educated than Pentecostals. People who drink vintage champagne tend to have higher household incomes than people who drink Night Train. A vast amount of research—both market studies and leisure time surveys—confirms the reality of cultural stratification.

The link between cultural taste and socioeconomic position is not always straightforward, however. Many cultural objects—detective novels and popular television programs, for example—cut across class, regional, ethnic, and gender boundaries. For this reason, Herbert Gans (1974) proposed that we designate the audience or recipients of any cultural object as taste cultures, without making any assumptions about their social or demographic characteristics. Moreover, social strata differ in the breadth of their cultural participation. To put it simply, upper middle-class and middle-class people do more of everything than working-class people. Thus, whereas a working-class man may be knowledgeable about sports, popular music, and television, his middle-class counterpart is likely to be knowledgeable about fine arts, classical music, serious fiction, *and* sports, popular music, and television, to the extent that Peterson called high-status middle-class groups "cultural omnivores" (1992; see also DiMaggio, 1987). This broader cultural repertoire allows the middle-class person to operate in a variety of social settings, switching his or her presentation of cultural knowledge to suit the occasion. In sharp contrast, one of the deprivations of ghetto dwellers is that although they may understand and adroitly negotiate the complex system of signification in which they live, their cultural skills are not transferable to the world outside the ghetto (Wilson, 1987). Unlike middle-class and, to a lesser extent, working-class people, ghetto dwellers cannot code-switch, for they have had little interactive experience with other cultures. So just as people do not altogether choose the "taste cultures" in which they participate, neither do they choose the consequences.

A powerful theory of the consequences of taste has been put forward by French sociologist Pierre Bourdieu (1984), who argues that culture may be thought of as capital. Like economic capital, cultural capital can be accumulated and invested; moreover, it can be converted into economic capital. Take a simple example: Two workers, on the basis of job performance, are equally qualified for a promotion. Their boss is an enthusiast for Japanese culture; she has scrolls and wedding kimonos on the walls of her office, she reads modern Japanese fiction, she enjoys going out for sushi. Worker A is able to talk with her about a favorite Mishima novel or the merits of a new sushi bar. Worker B lacks the cultural capital—the background of knowledge and taste—to pick up on and respond to his boss's interest (or, even worse, he is heard to mutter something about the revolting thought of eating raw fish). All else being equal, which worker is more likely to develop a friendly relationship with the boss and get promoted?

Bourdieu mapped out the relationship between economic capital and cultural capital. Sometimes they correspond, as in the case of wealthy people who are able to purchase and patronize the fine arts, but at other times economic and cultural capital are at odds. Students, for example, are often high on cultural capital but low on economic; poorly educated but financially successful entrepreneurs or blue-collar workers may be high on economic capital and low on cultural. These latter usually try to raise the cultural capital of their children by seeing that they get a good education, preferably at prestigious schools.

Although economic capital may be bolstered, increased, or undercut by forms of noneconomic capital, the types of readily negotiable noneconomic capital may vary from place to place. After studying middle-class Frenchmen and Americans living in two major cities (Paris and New York) and two provincial towns (Clermont-Ferrand and Indianapolis), Michèle Lamont (1992) found that the kind of cultural capital Bourdieu stressed—knowledge of the arts, refinement of taste—was more important in Paris than in any of the other locations. In provincial towns, what might be termed moral capital—a reputation for honesty, decency, reliability—is more important in deciding who is admirable. And Americans generally respect money, sheer economic capital, more than the French do.

Although exquisite taste and appreciation of artistic genres may be particularly Parisian, research indicates that possessing or not possessing cultural capital can explain a variety of social stratification outcomes. For example, let us say that getting a college degree and a well-educated spouse are both "prizes" valued by a given society. Let us further imagine that people having the same amount of wealth but different amounts of cultural capital (measured by such indicators as attendance at arts and musical events or reading serious literature) are competing for these prizes. DiMaggio and Mohr (1985) showed that those individuals having high amounts of cultural capital are more likely to win both the degree and the educated mate than their less culturally sophisticated counterparts.

Because people believe that cultural capital matters, there is a natural tendency for groups to inflate the value of what they already possess and to try to prevent other groups from getting any. Historian Lawrence Levine (1988) documented how upper-class white Americans, feeling threatened by new immigrant groups, segregated their cultural institutions as "high culture," to be supported and honored by everyone but not to be too available to the masses, who might misbehave. Museums and other high-cultural bastions of this period often were not open on weekends and evenings, for example, ensuring that those who had to work for a living couldn't make much use of them. (Again recall those lions guarding the doorways of art museums and libraries.) Similarly, Nicola Beisel (1990) showed how the same elites used anti-vice laws to make certain forms of popular entertainment, such as burlesque, illegitimate.

It seems clear that the reception of various types of cultural objects is often stratified by social class and that people may consciously or unconsciously use culture to support their social advantages or overcome their disadvantages. Our next step is to consider how an understanding of stratified recipients can be related to cultural objects as meaningful, shared symbols embodied in forms.

Horizons of Expectations

A German literary critic named Hans Robert Jauss provided a key for sociologists trying to understand cultural reception. Helping formulate the theory of literary reception aesthetics in the 1970s, Jauss (1982) pointed out that when a reader picks up a book, she does not come to it as an empty vessel waiting to be filled by its contents. Instead, she locates it against a "horizon of expectations" shaped by her previous literary, cultural, and social experience. A reader interprets the text—finds meaning in it—on the basis of how it fits or challenges her expectations. In constructing the text's meaning, she finds her horizon of expectations changing as well.

Jauss's reception aesthetics makes it possible to link the cultural and the social in the process of meaning construction. For example, in a study of how readers (book reviewers and literary critics) from three places interpreted the novels of a writer from Barbados named George Lamming, I found that different audiences interpreted the same books in very different ways (Griswold, 1987). West Indian readers said Lamming's autobiographical novel *In the Castle of My Skin* was about the ambiguities of identity; the British readers said it was about how a youth, any youth, comes to maturity; American readers said it was about race. Given their differing horizons of expectations, and given the complexity and ambiguity of the novel, three related but distinct sets of meanings emerged among the three categories of recipients.

The concept of a horizon of expectations extends well beyond literature and offers a way to understand how any cultural object may be interpreted by people with specific types of social and cultural knowledge and experience. More than this, it suggests how any event may be transformed into a cultural object by being made meaningful. Of particular interest to sociologists is the additional virtue that this model offers rich comparative possibilities. Consider what would at first seem to be not a cultural object at all but a brutal factual event: the death of a child. In the United States, such an event is generally regarded as utterly tragic, a horrible accident, an intrusion of chaos into the predictability of our lives. The very meaninglessness of such a death can be made meaningful—rendered a cultural object—by setting it against our horizon of expectations about babies: Babies are individually valuable, cherished, and rarely die. Thus, the death of an infant is a horrifying anomaly, defying all normal expectations.

In a Brazilian slum, on the other hand, a child's death has a different meaning altogether. Anthropologist Nancy Scheper-Hughes (1992) showed how parents in the squalid settlements outside a city in northeastern Brazil set infant mortality against a horizon shaped by extreme poverty, violence, powerlessness, and the ordinary event of children dying before they have begun to live. Given this horizon, these mothers (and sometimes fathers, though the men are often absent) respond to a child's death with fatalism and an almost complete lack of emotion. These Brazilian parents regard their babies and young as potential human beings, not real ones. For people with such a horizon, an infant's death doesn't mean "One of our children has died," but "A creature that was never fated to live (who lacked the 'knack for living' the Brazilians say) has departed. He was an angel, not a human, and has returned to Heaven."

Looking at the different interpretations that people construct from the same cultural objects may reveal deeply held social assumptions. If we think of a television show as "shared meaning embodied in form," for example, we find that different groups of people share different horizons and therefore construct different shared meanings from the same cultural object. Tamara Leibes and Elihu Katz (1990) studied the way groups of viewers in Israel interpreted the prime-time soap opera *Dallas*. Moroccan Jews who had immigrated to Israel saw *Dallas* as being about the bonds of kinship and how difficult family life could sometimes be. Russian emigrants interpreted the series as a straightforward, none-too-subtle critique of capitalism. And native-born Israelis, just like a control group in Los Angeles, did not regard the program as reflecting any social reality at all; for them it was simply slick television entertainment.

By now the question arises: If every group has its own distinctive horizon of expectations, can such groups of people construct any meanings they please? Can cultural objects be interpreted in any way whatsoever, or do the form and content of cultural objects constrain the meanings that can be found in them? Both the academic world and the general public have vigorously debated this question, which essentially concerns how much freedom cultural receivers have as meaning makers. Let us examine this ongoing controversy.

Freedom of Cultural Interpretation: Two Views

At the point where human beings experience cultural objects, they have reactions, construct interpretations, make meanings. We have seen that different groups can construct somewhat different meanings out of the same cultural objects. But how much freedom do people have to make these meanings?

Theoretically, there could be two opposing answers: (1) People can make any meanings whatsoever (receivers are strong/cultural objects are weak) and (2) people must submit to whatever meanings are inherently contained in the cultural object (cultural objects are strong/receivers are weak). At one extreme is unlimited freedom: People can do anything they want with the cultural objects they receive. The French structuralist Claude Lévi-Strauss (1966) once referred to the human mind as like a bricoleur or tinkerer, the sort of handyman who could fix things, make things, out of whatever bits and scraps of material happened to be around. Following this bricoleur logic, the recipient of a cultural object can make meanings virtually independent of the cultural object itself. We've all heard jokes to this effect: A sixteen-year-old boy asks another what a particular book is about, and he replies, "It's about sex." He is then asked what the movie he saw last night was about; "Oh, it was about sex, too." And so on.

Presumably this young man would find a bowl of cereal, a passage from *The Merchant of Venice*, or a trip to the Laundromat to be "about sex."

This view, however—the view that recipients can make cultural objects mean anything, that virtually any bit of culture can be "about sex" or about anything else—denies autonomy to cultural objects themselves. It implies that there are no distinctions, no better or worse, richer or poorer, inspirational or depressing, elevating or pornographic cultural representations, only different kinds of people experiencing the cultural object and imputing different meanings to it. Meaning becomes entirely a function of the receiver's mind. Such a position is anathema to a traditional humanities-based approach to culture (though it is held by some contemporary literary critics). Social scientists are uncomfortable with it as well, for it denies culture's role as a collective representation. If anything goes, if any person's interpretation is as good as the next, then culture's capacity to serve as a means whereby people "communicate, perpetuate, and develop their knowledge about and attitude toward life" is undermined.

The other extreme position holds that cultural meanings are tightly controlled and that receivers have virtually no freedom of interpretation. According to this view, people ignorant about the conventions of a particular cultural object may not understand it, outsiders to a subculture may not "get it," scholars and specialists may labor to ferret out the hidden meaning of a text or symbol, but there is *a* meaning. Such a conviction, which for many people seems no more than common sense, has been called the "proper meaning superstition." Even though a cultural creator may aim for a particular interpretation or response to a work, our own experience suggests that people vary enormously in their responses to a cultural object. Recall Baxandall's concept of a period eye. We might suppose that every period, and every group within a particular period, has a somewhat different "eye." One man (a merchant) looks at a heap of gold in a painting and gauges how much gold is in the pile, another (a jeweler) assesses its quality based on color, and a third viewer (an unmarried woman) thinks of the value of her dowry. Each viewer's eye is conditioned by his or her social placement, and this seems to be the case regardless of what the painter intended. Different viewers, different meanings.

When we push these positions to their logical extremes in this way, neither one seems justified. Two schools of thought in the social sciences, however, essentially represent these extremes in somewhat more presentable form. The first, mass culture theory, leans toward the strong culture/weak receivers side, suggesting that cultural objects can essentially overwhelm their helpless recipients. The second, popular culture theory, sees people not as helpless in the face of the cultural onslaught, but as active makers and manipulators of meaning. These two schools offer very different conceptions of how human freedom and cultural power relate. Assumptions from each pop up in the public discourse over, for example, the influence of news media on presidential elections or the effects of lewd lyrics in popular songs. We need, therefore, to examine their assumptions and sort out their implications.

Seduction by Mass Culture

In my earlier discussion of the production of culture, the expression "culture industry" referred to the organizations that produced cultural objects for a market. It was a neutral term, implying neither good nor bad. In the view of mass culture theorists, however, there is little good about the culture industry.

Those who adopt the mass culture perspective see the culture industry as the technology for producing mass entertainment on a hitherto undreamed-of scale. Such entertainment aims at a low common denominator of taste, emphasizing the lurid over the moral or intellectual, in order to capture as wide a market as possible. Mass cultural products render their recipients numb and apathetic. This apathy, in turn, leaves these passive recipients ripe for political tyranny, while their sheer numbers force cultural producers to come up with ever more violent, sensational, shocking materials to get a response from their jaded audience.

We have seen this view before as far back as Plato, and more recently from the Frankfurt school. During the 1950s, when television was transforming cultural participation in the United States and Europe, criticism of mass culture came from both the political Left and the Right. The Left saw the capacity for political criticism buried under the mindless drivel of mass entertainments; the Right saw the capacity for cultural critique, for refinement of taste, buried. Both Right and Left agreed that independent thought was imperiled, both worried about media-induced brainwashing, and both drew dark historical parallels with Roman emperors who diverted the plebeians with "bread and circuses" while the empire crumbled.

Of particular concern was the impact that mass culture might have on children, who were assumed to be impressionable and vulnerable to its messages. A typical specimen of this school was *Seduction of the Innocent* (1954), a book written by clinical psychologist Frederic Wertham, with excerpts appearing in *Ladies' Home Journal*. The subject was comic books, especially those depicting crime. Wertham was horrified by children's exposure to this mass cultural product: "Children spend an inordinate amount of time with comic books, many of them two or three hours a day. . . . How can you get the 'total picture' of a child when you leave out entirely what occupies him two or three hours a day?" (p. 11). He castigated comics for contributing to illiteracy, delinquency, and sexual perversion, as well as for glorifying violence as a means of solving problems. He was especially outraged by the interplay of the comics' messages about violence and sexuality with their advertisements:

> Comic-book stories teach violence, the advertisements provide the weapons. The stories instill a wish to be a superman, the advertisements promise to supply the means for becoming one. Comic-book heroines have super-figures; the comic-book advertisements promise to develop them. . . . The stories feature scantily clad girls; the advertisements outfit peeping Toms. (p. 217)

In such an indictment, we recognize the effects cited by the Frankfurt school (numbing and incitement to mindless violence), as well as the degradation, brutalization, and sexual explicitness deplored by conservative thinkers.

Although the violence and sexual explicitness of contemporary mass culture make Wertham's worries about comic books seem downright quaint, the concern with mass culture's possible negative effects has remained. From the early 1970s until the present, for example, many sociologists have examined how mass cultural products perpetuated racial and gender stereotypes. A current example of this type of research focuses on children's books. Although these stories have gotten rid of the more obvious forms of gender bias and now offer stories featuring little girls almost as often as little boys, animal characters continue to be masculine by an astonishing ratio of six to one (Grauerholz & Pescosolido, 1989). Because animal protagonists—plucky, smart, adventuresome, full of desirable character traits—are extremely popular with young children, this pattern may perpetuate biased assumptions about gender (e.g., plucky, smart, adventuresome, desirable people are male) in a more subtle version than the old Dick-and-Jane stereotypes.

Mass culture's relation to violence is another evergreen topic, as in the legal actions involving rap singers, whose music seems to many people to promote violence toward the police and toward women. Popular music and especially television receive constant scrutiny for their impact on their audiences, particularly on children, although such scrutiny has had little inhibiting effect on the culture industry. Counterarguments cite freedom of expression, market demands, and the fact that mass culture only "reflects" the culture at large. In the view of mass culture critics, however, no horizon of expectations is robust enough to withstand the constant onslaught of violence and perversion. All audiences, they believe, are innocent, and all can be seduced.

The opposite view, however, holds that people are too knowing, too canny to be led down the garden path by cultural objects. This view speaks not of mass, but of popular culture.

Resistance Through Popular Culture

In some ways, the term popular culture is a redundancy. Culture is public, and all culture must be popular to some extent; unpopular culture, like a TV pilot that fails to attract an audience, just goes away. But the term has come to mean the culture of the people, and here *people* means the common people, the non-elite majority—hence the commonly heard contrast between high culture (or serious culture, or good culture, or Culture) and popular culture.

Popular culture clearly includes mass cultural products such as television shows, popular magazines, and off-the-rack fashions. It also includes, and emphasizes, the wisdom, the common sense, the values, the way of life of "the people," especially the nonpowerful, nonwealthy—those groups who, according to Bourdieu, lack both economic and cultural capital. In this respect, it draws on the old anthropological "way-of-life" definitions of culture. As indicated in the Snow and Anderson (1993) study of the homeless, all people need meaning in their lives; meaningfulness is not just a luxury indulged in by the well-to-do, but a human necessity. Popular culture, so the theory goes, is the system of meanings available to ordinary people.

Among sociologists, the reevaluation of popular culture began in the 1960s, when previously dominated and ignored groups—minorities, gays, women, the poor—were demanding respect as never before. Now many social scientists, as well as scholars in the humanities, felt uncomfortable with the old attitudes that soap operas for women were trivial, black English was substandard, or the practices of the poor were irrational and dysfunctional. Scholars examining previously despised works, genres, and systems of meaning found them to contain complexities and beauties; at the same time, deconstructing previously esteemed works, genres, and systems of meaning, they found widespread representations of class hegemony, patriarchy, and illegitimate canonization.

The reevaluation of popular culture occurred in two ways, and both of these approaches involve an image of the audience that is far from passive. First, scholars examined popular culture itself in search of hidden meanings, meanings that had been accessible to its recipients but missed by academics and other disdainful elites. For example, in separate studies Tanya Modleski ([1982] 1984) and Janice Radway (1984) took a new look at an almost universally scorned form of popular literature, women's romance novels. Radway, who used focus groups to talk with readers about their interpretations of the romances, discovered they had distinct criteria for assessing the quality of what was usually dismissed as homogeneous formulaic novels. Moreover, the novels themselves were seen to contain a theme of the male who moves from arrogance to nurturing. This nurturing male was especially attractive to women readers, who typically were nurturers themselves and longed to be cared for in kind. Modleski found Harlequin romances to contain a revenge theme—the heroine almost dies or otherwise abandons the hero, causing him pain until she returns—and suggested that this subject represented women's collective fantasy of getting back at their oppressors. In both studies, and in this type of analysis as a whole, the popular audience is seen as decoding meanings that are especially satisfying in light of its social experience.

In the second form of reevaluating popular culture, the recipient is seen not only as decoding meanings to which elite recipients have been oblivious, but also as actively constructing subversive meanings. Mass cultural objects may indeed be patriarchal or represent the "ideas of the ruling class," as the theory goes, but people do not have to accept these meanings imposed, as it were, from outside. They make their own meanings.

John Fiske (1989) used the analogy of mass culture being like a supermarket. People may pick up mass-produced items from the cultural supermarket, but when they cook (make meanings), they mix these supermarket goods with whatever they have in the pantry at home, thereby individualizing and transforming the final product. The results can be surprising. For example, Fiske studied audience reactions to *The Newlywed Game*, a television game show wherein couples scored points when each could accurately predict the other's responses to questions, which usually had risqué overtones. Although couples who exhibited high levels of agreement were the winners in the program's formal terms, it was the losers—those who disagreed with each other—who won roars of approval from the audience. Fiske saw this reaction as a case of people creating counterhegemonic cultural objects and subversive meanings. The rules of the game supported marital harmony under generally patriarchal authority, but the audience cheered for the rebels.

Both the popular culture theorists like Fiske and the mass culture theorists like Wertham are essentially concerned with reception, and both

Figure 4-2

Mass Culture and Popular Culture Theories on the Cultural Diamond

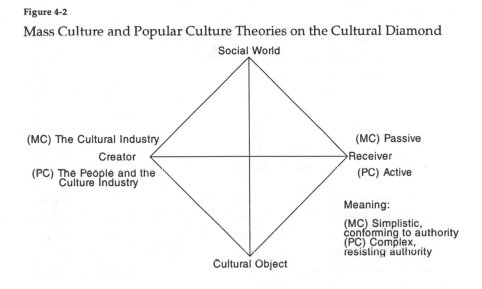

share the value of human freedom, but they interpret the relationship between cultural object and receiver very differently. Figure 4-2 presents a schematic of their differences on the cultural diamond. In the mass culture model, cultural objects impose their (simple, sensational) meanings on their audiences, but in the popular culture model, the audience makes new meanings.

As the global spread of mass communications technology increases, it remains to be seen which view of the cultural object/recipient relationship proves more accurate. Because cultural objects are interpreted not in isolation, but by interacting human beings, it seems likely that distinct interpretations, or reinterpretations, will continue to emerge from groups having distinct experiences. The real danger, not envisioned by either mass culture or popular culture theory, may be that people will stop interpreting cultural objects at all. Like the native-born Israelis and Los Angelenos in the study of *Dallas,* people bombarded with cultural objects may simply reject the idea that these objects are socially meaningful. This rejection has already happened, to some extent and with some cultural objects, and theorists of postmodern culture expect the trend to accelerate. We take up the prospect of abandoned meaning in Chapter 7. For now, suffice it to say that such an intellectual disengagement of the receivers of culture from the cultural objects themselves may be a far more frightening idea than anything that the mass culture theorists envisioned.

Summary

In this chapter, we have completed an exploration of the points and links of the culture diamond. Having already examined cultural objects and social meanings, and the collective creation of those objects, we have considered here the production-of-culture linkages among creators, objects, and recipients. We have considered the role of recipients themselves, who bear socially shaped horizons of expectations and are engaged, actively or passively, with the culture they experience. Either through their numbed passivity or their grass-roots power, these recipients, in turn, affect their social world.

Our analytic model is complete. But models themselves are no good unless they can tell us something about the world in which we live. In the next two chapters, we apply our analytic devices to social problems and to business and organizational transactions. In these two chapters, we observe with a sociologically informed eye the operation of cultural meanings in the real world and the influence they exert.

RECOMMENDED FOR FURTHER READING

Beisel, Nicola. 1990. "Class, Culture, and Campaigns Against Vice in Three American Cities, 1872-1892." *American Sociological Review* 55: 44-62. A fascinating historical account of how high-status groups tried to shore up their domination by suppressing the cultural tastes of subordinate groups.

Lamont, Michèle. 1992. *Money, Morals, and Manners: The Culture of the French and the American Upper-Middle Class.* Chicago: University of Chicago Press. A comparison of how the French and the Americans assign status to others on the basis of their cultural refinement, their integrity, and their wealth.

Peterson, Richard A., ed. 1976. *The Production of Culture.* Beverly Hills, CA: Sage. Studies of science, arts, and religion that demonstrate the production of culture approach.

Radway, Janice A. 1984. *Reading the Romance: Women, Patriarchy, and Popular Literature.* Chapel Hill: University of North Carolina Press. From the popular culture school, Radway takes seriously both romance novels and the women who read them. Using focus groups, she explores how the readers construct their own meanings and criteria for evaluation.

5

The Cultural Construction
of Social Problems

Poverty, crime, teenage pregnancy, high infant mortality rates, racism, urban decay, unemployment, drugs, drunk driving, inadequate health care—and on and on. Most of us can reel off a list of pressing social problems without hesitation. Although such a list has roots in problems that cause human suffering universally—such as violence, hatred, and premature death—the forms that these problems take are specific to each culture and society.

Americans regard teenage pregnancy as a social problem, for example. For the Hausa of Nigeria, where most girls marry at the age of 12 or 13, young women who reach their twenties *without* having at least one or two children constitute a social problem. For the Chinese, whose government is addressing its population problem by vigorously enforcing a one-child-per family policy, any pregnancy is problematic. If the family has no children, the problem is whether or not the baby will be a son (desirable) or a daughter (less desirable). Infant girls often show up abandoned near orphanages, left to the charity of strangers so that the parents can try for another pregnancy (virtually all babies in Chinese orphanages are females or severely handicapped males). If the family already has a child, the pregnancy must be hidden or else the mother may be forced to abort. Pregnancy, not teenage pregnancy in particular, is a social as well as an individual problem for the Chinese. So teenage pregnancy is a social problem whose contours are highly specific to the American context.

Even here, labeling "teenage pregnancy" as the problem may be misleading. Few Americans regard the pregnancy of a nineteen-year-old woman with a working husband as a problem, but such is the profile of many women included in statistics and stories about the "dramatic rise in teen pregnancy." After reviewing the statistics, Kristen Luker (1991) concluded that concerns about "babies having babies" have more to do with public disapproval of the welfare system, racial prejudices, and concerns about teenage sexual activity than they do with actual demographic changes. Moreover, the common assumption that early childbearing causes school dropout and poverty for the young mothers and their children is incorrect; the evidence that Luker examined suggests that it is the other way around.

We all recognize that certain cultural objects serve to focus attention on social problems, such as *The Jungle,* Upton Sinclair's indictment of the meat-packing industry that helped provoke passage of the Pure Food and Drug Act, or *Uncle Tom's Cabin,* Harriet Beecher Stowe's sensational depiction of the horrors of slavery that transfixed northern U.S. readers. Similarly, Yoruba theatrical troupes in Nigeria dramatize social inequities before rural audiences, and Chinese short-story writers depict the "bitter leaves" of their disappointment over recent economic, but not political, liberalization. But consider another possibility. If culture can draw attention to social problems, can it also sometimes create the problem? And if so, what might be the role of culture in the solution of these problems it has helped bring about?

A key point, obviously, is the degree to which social problems are culturally constructed in the first place. We begin this chapter with a consideration of social problems as another form of cultural object. We then turn to a series of events labeled as social problems—inequality, the dislocations of modernity, conflicts involving race and ethnicity,—and apply a cultural diamond as a way of shedding light on these troubling issues.

Making Trouble:
The Rise and Fall of Social Problems

We have seen that culture imposes meanings on an otherwise chaotic and random universe. Cultural systems turn events and objects into cultural objects with meanings specific to each culture; a business card is meaningful to a Japanese in a way that it is not to an American. In just this way, we can see how certain phenomena in the social world are made meaningful, transformed into cultural objects and, more specifically, into social problems.

Consider what takes place when things that "just happen" become cultural objects. We have all seen the fatalistic bumper stickers that proclaim "Shit happens." The world *is* full of painful occurrences, private tragedies, large-scale and persistent deprivations; life is neither fair nor kind or naturally and obviously meaningful. Sometimes, though, the human misery that "happens" is transformed from a mere happening into a meaningful cultural object, and the cultural object gets designated as a social problem. When this transformation takes place, it becomes possible for people to seek solutions, for the existence of a "problem" implies the existence of a "solution." (Thus, we do not regard death as a "problem," for it has no "solution.")

What happens when we see poverty as a social problem in the United States? In this case, it becomes a cultural object read against a horizon of expectations (e.g., America is a rich country), interpreted (e.g., given our abundance, America should not have any significant poverty), assumed to have a creator (e.g., what are the forces and actions that shape this cultural object of American poverty?), and seen as something to be overcome (e.g., with a "War on Poverty," Lyndon Johnson's program of the 1960s). If poverty is not seen as a social problem—the poor are always with us—then its more painful consequences can be alleviated, but poverty itself is not seen as something to be solved. Considered as a cultural object, on the other hand, poverty (and any other social problem) can benefit from the same type of cultural diamond analysis as any other cultural object, asking who creates the definition of the problem, who receives and interprets it, what meanings does it contain, and what is the social world in which it is meaningful.

From Happening to Event to Social Problem

First, let's consider how "happenings" turn into "cultural objects." The creation of a cultural object is like the creation of an event, which anthropologist Marshall Sahlins (1985) describes as the relationship between a happening and a structure, a relationship created by interpretation. How do happenings become cultural objects identified as social problems? It appears that for a cultural object first to be created and then to be identified as a social problem, it must articulate with an interlocking set of ideas and institutions. Schematically, this process looks like Figure 5-1.

Consider the social problem that Americans identify as the drunk driver, a case that sociologist Joseph Gusfield (1981) examined closely. The relevant set of happenings might include: auto accidents; traffic fatalities; all accidental deaths, especially those involving young people; alcohol use and abuse; transportation patterns, including the American reliance on cars and the underfunding of public transportation; car design that emphasizes style or affordability over safety (as in manufacturers' reluctance to install air bags); and American individualism, including an attitude that seat belts are a nuisance or limit one's personal freedom. How is it, asked Gusfield, that out of all these phenomena, all these happenings,

Figure 5-1

Transforming Happenings Into Cultural Objects

the American people have singled out the "drunk driver" as the single meaningful cultural object and social problem?

The answer lies in American ideas and institutions. Our culture emphasizes individual responsibility. Therefore, a tragedy such as a fatal accident must be some individual's fault; blaming it on "the system" is not the American way. We have a history of temperance movements and prohibition, as well as a lingering association of alcohol with immorality (taxes on liquor and cigarettes are routinely referred to as "sin taxes"). The flip side of our emphasis on personal freedom (with the car and the open road emblematic of this emphasis) is our belief in personal control. Drunkenness is individually "sinful" in two ways: The individual has made a bad decision (to get drunk; to drink and drive), and she has given up her ability to control herself, her body, her car. Hence the concept of the "killer drunk" fits a number of strands in our common web of ideas. It fits our institutions as well. Powerful industries such as auto manufacturers and liquor distillers support the construction of the "problem" as poor individual decision making, rather than booze or unsafe (or too many) cars. And our legal system is better equipped to take on individuals who may have committed criminal acts than to go after organizations or systems (though in recent years, class action suits have made inroads).

Even the response to auto fatalities fits the ideological and institutional context. Mothers Against Drunk Driving (MADD) has been highly effective in getting tougher laws on the books and enforced. The very name of this organization sets up a morality play pitting the mother defending her young against the villainous drunk driver who imperils them. It also forecloses debate (who would be *for* drunk driving?) and helps perpetuate the construction of a social problem in such a way that certain solutions (e.g., better public transportation, a high tax on gasoline) are rendered unthinkable. And within MADD itself, members accord the highest prestige to women who have actually lost children in auto accidents involving drunk drivers. A mother grieving for a dead child is a tremendously powerful image in many predominantly Christian societies, not because Christian mothers love their children more than other mothers, but because the image of the *pietà*—Mary holding the dead Christ—is a familiar cultural icon. This symbol of maternal grief evoked by MADD focuses attention squarely on individuals—individuals who drink, drive, kill, die, grieve, and act—and not on organizations or systems.

In Nigeria, death on the highway is also an event and a cultural object, but its meaning within the cultural system is quite different. A deadly combination of deteriorated roads, nonexistent traffic law enforcement, crowded conditions, uninhibited drivers, and vehicles that are often overloaded and poorly maintained give rise to enormous carnage on the roads, a fact that all Nigerians acknowledge. The Nobel Prize-winning playwright Wole Soyinka has made danger on the highways a recurring theme in his plays. But Nigerians don't point to the drivers, the pedestrians, or the vehicles as the social problem; for them, the problem is "the road." In Nigerian culture, the road is always a place of danger as well as excitement, a place where witches and destructive spirits lurk to trap the unwary (Bastian, 1992). Ben Okri's novel *The Famished Road* (1991) tells of a road that actually devours its victims. As Gusfield (1981) would point out, by defining a public problem in such a way—constructing it as a cultural object with meanings involving spirits and fate—the Nigerians are focusing attention on some types of solutions (placate the spirits; don't travel) and not on others (fix the roads; build sidewalks).

Thus social problems tend to show a comfortable fit with the ideas and institutions of the society in which they are found. For this reason, public problems are generally constructed in one way, and not in other equally plausible ways; this is why "teenage pregnancy" is the problem in the U.S., not "teenagers in poverty" or "restricted availability of contraception." Witches are a social problem in Nigeria because the surrounding culture contains a set of ideas that support a belief in witchcraft, a set of remedies to counter a witch's influence, and a set of institutions, including media—especially the tabloid press, always eager to spread the word about new cases of witchcraft—and markets eager to trade in remedies against bewitching. Suspected witches are killed, as are innocent people (often children) who are killed in order to make medicine against witches. As the sociologist W. I. Thomas (1966) pointed out long ago, if people define a situation as real, it is real in its consequences.

The Career of a Social Problem

If social problems are culturally defined, it stands to reason that problems wax and wane in popularity over time. Stephen Hilgartner and Charles Bosk (1988) tried to identify what accounts for the "rise and fall of social problems," beginning with what gets identified as a social problem in the first place. These authors envision a public arena in which competition takes place among the conditions that potentially could be labeled as social problems. This competition occurs in two forms: (1) in the framing or definition of the problem itself (e.g., Is the problem one of drunk drivers or of overreliance on automobiles?) and (2) in capturing the attention of institutions—government, media, foundations—that have limits on their resources or "carrying capacities." Those conditions that get selected as social problems are phenomena that have specific characteristics: They are or can be made dramatic; they resonate with deep mythic themes in the culture; and they are politically viable, often because they are linked with powerful interest groups. Winners in this competition achieve the status of widely acknowledged social problems.

Consider the AIDS epidemic as an example. In the early 1980s, it became clear to epidemiologists and to some members of the homosexual men's community in a few cities that a new, highly contagious, and invariably fatal disease involving the collapse of the immune system was spreading widely. Yet it was several years before public arenas—including federal and local government, the medical establishment, and much of the gay community itself—took alarm and identified AIDS as a major social problem (Shilts, 1987). Within the American gay subculture, a strong emphasis on sexual freedom as political expressiveness meant that, for some time, medical warnings about safe sex fell on deaf ears. The disease was highly dramatic, especially in the wasting away of its youthful victims, but few media outlets exploited its dramatic potential at first, for it was believed to be confined to members of a stigmatized group. The same was true outside the United States. For several years, governments in East Africa were reluctant to address AIDS, despite its epidemic proportions in their countries, because they associated the disease with male homosexual behavior, which Africans consider to be abhorrent. Because of this association, the disease was "culturally impossible" and therefore did not merit recognition as a social problem.[1] In both East Africa and the United

[1] AIDS became "possible" in East African countries only with the recognition that prostitution apparently is the primary transmission mechanism for the disease in Africa. Prostitution is far more socially acceptable than homosexuality in most African cultures.

States, AIDS did not initially resonate with mythic themes, nor did it link up with powerful political actors; indeed, quite the opposite.

As Hilgartner and Bosk might predict, once AIDS could no longer be ignored, there was competition over the very definition of the "problem": Was it AIDS, sexual promiscuity, or (as some religious conservatives claimed) homosexuality itself? Although the struggle over problem definition was fierce, the gay men's viewpoint was helped by their high level of education, political savvy, and access to the arts and media. By the mid-1980s, gay men and their supporters had dramatized the epidemic in highly effective ways, through the NAMES Project AIDS Quilt, through plays such as *The Normal Heart* that reached a liberal and affluent constituency, through books such as Randy Shilts's *And the Band Played On*, and through public rituals, such as releasing hundreds of balloons for each AIDS death, that offered good visuals for the evening news. Celebrities helped, both those who died of AIDS (Rock Hudson, Liberace, Michael Foucault, Perry Ellis, Arthur Ashe) and those who used their prominence to urge support for AIDS research (Elizabeth Taylor). Not only did the gay men's associations engage in lobbying, but the rapid spread of the disease and its identification with non-gay populations also removed the stigma associated with it; if "normal, decent people" could get AIDS from a routine blood transfusion, then it became everybody's problem. Under the conservative Reagan administration, the U.S. Surgeon General sent a brochure to every household regarding safe sex, and condoms moved off the pharmacy's back shelf and into the limelight. Media attention continues to be intense and crucial, as in a notorious Benetton advertisement showing not the firm's clothes, but a family embracing a young man dying of AIDS (the pietà motif again). Some AIDS activists are concerned, however, that AIDS spread among intravenous drug users—another stigmatized group, like gays—coupled with its low incidence outside these two groups will eventually reduce its saliency as a social problem.

The career of AIDS offers a clear example of how cultural values and themes shape (or obstruct) the very definition of a social problem. The social problem itself is a cultural object, with those who produce or create it (as a social problem), those who constitute its public or audience, and a set of meanings that interpreters use to relate it to the social world. Not all social problems appear with the relative suddenness of AIDS, however. Some, such as poverty or crime, are always present but rise and fall in terms of public attention. Others are associated with long-term structural changes, such as modernization, and may only gain attention when they generate countermovements in response. In the rest of this chapter, we examine a series of social problems involving (1) inequality, (2) racial and ethnic conflict, and (3) the fundamentalist response to modernity to see how the creation and reception of "cultural objects" play a role in each.

The Cultural Reproduction of Inequality

During the heyday of functionalist sociology in the 1950s and 1960s, the relationship between culture and economic development seemed to be clear. As societies modernized, functionalists believed, certain cultural changes appeared—changes that stretched from individual personalities to large-scale institutions. These changes were seen as including the following:

- A shift from ascriptive to achievement criteria. In a modern society, a person would get a job because of merit, not because she was the boss's sister.

- A shift from group or kinship-based solidarity to individualism. This shift was exemplified in the choice of marriage partner, in which individual preference would replace family arrangements.

- A shift from local or provincial to cosmopolitan orientation. People would become aware of the outside world through media and would orient their behavior and thinking to outside events.

Underlying the identification of these changes was the assumption that modern industrialized societies were converging toward a common state of development. The West had gotten there first, but other countries and societies would catch up, and in the end all "developed societies" would resemble each other.

This assumption of convergence carried with it a number of implications regarding the connection between culture and economic inequality, either among nations or within them. Some of these were based on Weber's theory of the Protestant ethic. If Calvinist Protestantism had been the cultural root of economic change in the West, then scholars and policy-makers sought its equivalent in other societies (conversely, they cited its absence as reason for delayed development). In general, they tended to deem the cultural patterns of less economically developed nations as dysfunctional, requiring drastic change before they could make the leap into modernity.

Closer to home, social scientists told a parallel account of dysfunctional cultures: the culture of poverty. This thesis argued that poor communities and people developed cultural patterns that hampered their economic advancement. For example, families lacking a refrigerator might get into the habit of buying milk in small amounts—pints or half-pints—because larger quantities would spoil before they were used up. Even after the family acquired a refrigerator, the habit of buying in small volume might continue. But because milk is more expensive (per ounce) in small quantities than in quarts or half-gallons, this cultural pattern was dysfunctional; it meant that the poor continued to pay more for their milk.

In the 1970s, functionalist assumptions were sharply challenged and, in many respects, set aside. To many sociologists, convergence theories seemed like ethnocentric glorifications of the West for which there was little justification. To look for convergence to Western individualism, for example, was to miss what was actually going on in rapidly developing societies such as Japan. According to one influential argument, Japan's distinctive cultural patterns—such as subordination of individualism to the good of the group or the paternalism that encouraged lifetime employment—actually provided the basis for its growth as one of the "late developing" industrial societies (Dore, 1973).

More often, however, social scientists dismissed cultural obstacles or aids to economic change altogether. Structural factors—economic, demographic, political—became the new explanation for economic outcomes. An influential example of this kind of structuralist thinking was world system theory, which argued that history had produced a system in which agriculturally based countries on the "periphery" provided cheap raw materials to, and bought finished products from, industrially based countries in the "center." This was a stable arrangement, highly advantageous to the dominant "center" countries, and no cultural change in the periphery was likely to undo it.

A parallel movement took place in poverty research at home. Culture of poverty arguments now seemed to be "blaming the victim." To speak of "dysfunctional" cultural patterns, such as family practices, sexual norms, and work attitudes, was to invite harsh criticism from those who argued that structural factors—employment, educational opportunity, health care —were the keys to alleviating poverty.

By the 1990s, however, the issue of domestic poverty, especially the intractable problems associated with the urban underclass, made the more dogmatic structure-versus-culture arguments obsolete in their single-mindedness. Influential urban poverty scholars such as William Julius Wilson (1987) were now pointing out the destructive interplay between structural and cultural factors. Wilson argued, for example, that when segregation had forced all African Americans to live in the same neighborhoods, middle-class and employed working-class residents helped their poorer neighbors both culturally (by symbolizing exemplary lives and providing role models for hard work, orderly families, and upward mobility) and structurally (by providing information about job opportunities). Once residential segregation was no longer legal, the more prosperous residents left the old urban neighborhood, often following job opportunities in the suburbs. Increasingly, those left behind in the ghettos of the inner city were the "truly disadvantaged," those with little education or employment prospects. This isolated community—the home of the so-called underclass—became increasingly cut off from the rest of society in both cultural and economic terms.

Functionalism had argued that cultural changes could lead to economic development, a reduction in poverty, and greater social equality. Subsequent structuralist arguments dismissed the role of culture. When neither development nor poverty reduction proceeded according to the optimistic scenarios of the 1960s, culture was rediscovered, this time by social scientists with a left-wing orientation. The thesis became: Culture perpetuates social inequality. In some ways, this is an ironic reversal, representing a dynamic version of Marx's old "ruling ideas are the ideas of the ruling class" thesis.

Some of the theoretical bases for the new viewpoint come from those who study education. Basil Bernstein (1971), for example, discovered that children from working-class backgrounds came to school with linguistic disadvantages in comparison with middle-class children. Middle-class children came from households having a "elaborated code" of language in which abstract terms and complex verbal constructions were common. Working-class children, in contrast, were equipped with "restricted codes" emphasizing the concrete, the here-and-now. These children were less able to appropriate, make use of, and even make sense of the educational messages of the classroom, which assumed possession of an elaborated code. So even if middle-class and working-class children were in the same classes with the same teachers, the former would outperform the latter, and the difference would be likely to increase over time. (We saw in Chapter 3 how Bourdieu referred to a comparable phenomenon in his discussion of cultural capital.)

Early education, then, offers an example of how cultural and structural factors reinforce one another. In much of the United States, the poor child comes to school with a restricted linguistic code, limited cultural capital, often linguistic disadvantages (e.g., because of ghetto isolation, a limited exposure to "standard" English), and little familiarity with books or computers, standard tools of instruction. These are cultural liabilities. She also comes to school with no breakfast, anxiety caused by the sound of gunfire in her neighborhood, and some cognitive disabilities associated with poor prenatal and neonatal health care. These are structural liabilities. The new poverty research emphasizes that both of these elements must be addressed.

Cultural patterns may not only perpetuate inequality but also set up "moods and motivations" in people whereby they freely choose behaviors that in the long run will hurt them economically. Examples include the black student who avoids success in school for fear his friends will think he's "acting white," the girl who shrinks from studying math because she has received the cultural message that a career in engineering is not feminine, the Latino whose facility in Spanish and pride in his Mexican heritage make him unwilling to learn sufficient English to meet his high school's requirements. British sociologist Paul Willis ([1977] 1981) closely observed working-class boys in a tough Midlands school and revealed the development of a strong youth culture that steered students away from mental jobs and toward physical jobs. The "lads" participated in a rich, unofficial subculture that opposed the school's official cultural messages about hard work and self-improvement, equated mental work with femininity, and expressed mocking contempt for the "ear 'oles," those students who played by the rules. Their cultural dichotomies, or what Willis calls an ordered set of meanings, looked like Figure 5-2. The result was that the "lads" chose to leave school early in favor of employment in manual labor, thereby perpetuating their lower-class positions. But Willis gives an ironic spin to his account by suggesting that these young men have actually penetrated the ideological mystification of upward mobility. They knew, as the ear 'oles didn't, that even conformity and hard work in school were unlikely to improve their class positions, so they may as well "have a laff."

We have been considering culture's role in the reproduction of economic inequality here, but similar arguments have been made about other forms of inequality. An obvious subject is gender inequality, and an enormous amount of scholarship has documented how cultural patterns perpetuate women's subordinate economic and political status. Examples from other cultures—the Chinese practice of female infanticide or the Hausa practice of keeping married women secluded in the home—are glaring, but American culture provides plenty of examples as well. To take only one, Dorothy Holland and Margaret Eisenhart (1990) describe how men and women are "educated in romance" on American college campuses. The students are well versed in a cultural model of romance that emphasizes the ability to attract interest from members of the opposite sex, and they discuss and enact this model constantly. But "romance"

Figure 5-2

Official and Unofficial Culture in a British High School

Cultural system, from the Lads' viewpoint	School cultures	
	Official	*Unofficial*
Boys involved	Ear 'oles	Lads
Admired forms of labor	Mental	Physical
Gender identification	Feminine	Masculine
Attitude toward school rules	Conformist	Nonconformist
Attitude toward teachers	Docile, admiring	Rebellious, contemptuous
Attitude toward learning	Key to social mobility	A waste of time
Activity in school	Working, studying	"Having a laff" with Lads
When to leave school	At end of high school	As soon as legal
View of future	Upward mobility	Same life as parents

SOURCE: Adapted from Willis [1977] 1981

as a cultural object has different implications, different meanings, for men and women. Women gain prestige almost entirely through the men they attract, whereas men have a number of ways—including academic success and athletic success, as well as attractiveness to women—to gain status. Thus many women learn, rationally enough, to invest their time and energy into those attributes that pay off in their peer culture: personal attractiveness and winning male admiration. This strategy leads them to marginal careers, dissatisfaction with their college experiences, and "unfinished lives."

Cultural influences on economic inequality and gender roles are often confounded by another dimension, that of race or ethnicity. As we turn to these next, keep in mind that class, ethnicity, and gender—as in Luker's teenage pregnancy example—often combine in the cultural construction of social problems.

Race and Ethnicity as Cultural Objects

The sociological approach to race and ethnicity has undergone shifts comparable to, and in some cases directly related to, the shifts in its approach to inequality. The general convergence model was compatible with a view of eventual racial and ethnic assimilation, known in the United States as the melting pot, wherein ethnic and, ultimately, racial differences would disappear into a homogenized American identity. Outside this country, although the world was not seen as a huge melting pot, modernization theory did support the idea of Marshall McLuhan's "global village," in which media technology would link all humanity. In this view, ethnic and racial differences, and national boundaries as well, were growing less and less important.

In the 1960s, however, the social picture dramatically changed, both in the United States and abroad. At home, the civil rights movement brought African Americans' lack of assimilation to the forefront of American consciousness. Soon after, other ethnic groups—Native Americans, Poles, Italians, Hispanics, Irish—began asserting ethnic pride, emulating the assertiveness of the Black Pride rhetoric, and the old melting pot ideal no longer seemed either accurate or desirable. This change had parallels worldwide: Nationalist leaders of newly independent countries and the generation of political leaders that followed them rejected the convergence model and asserted their own distinctiveness. Third World nations declared their independence from either U.S. or Soviet domination, regardless of whether they were actually able to get along without support from one of the two big powers. In the 1970s, the human rights movement focused attention on the treatment of minority groups within nations. All of these new movements emphasized and even celebrated persistent ethnic differentiation.

Expressive culture played a major role in both American and foreign expressions of ethnic pride. If African leaders of the 1940s and 1950s wore suits from Savile Row and Paris as they negotiated with representatives of the colonial powers, the next generation of African leaders wore agbadas and other traditional dress. Often, however, they wore military uniforms, as political and economic changes proved more intractable than cultural changes. And cultural distinctiveness, often centered on differences in language and religion, tore apart many new nations as the old dreams of assimilation and convergence seemed more and more distant. By the 1990s, a number of countries such as Liberia and Bosnia-Herzegovina were being called "failed nations," and ethnic conflict was usually at the root of the failures.[2]

---

[2]Somalia is another nation often labeled as failed, but in this case, cultural distinctiveness seems to play no role. The rival groups, led by different warlords who may be from the same clan, share a religion, a language, and other cultural attributes. Once again, we are reminded how we need to understand the impact of both culture and structure on social processes; neither is sufficient by itself.

Cultural assertiveness, however—based on ethnicity, race, religion, language, or some combination of these—is likely to persist for a number of reasons and might be seen as a case of "cultural lead." First, its expression through cultural objects is psychologically satisfying yet often relatively low cost. An African American youth can wear a cap with a Malcolm X symbol or learn the intricacies of rap music more easily than he can effect change in his school, his neighborhood, or his job opportunities. Even when cultural allegiance is costly, as in the enmity between Protestant and Catholic in Northern Ireland or Serbs and Croats in the Balkans, it may be easier for an individual to apply simple rules of affiliation—she's a Serb, so she's my enemy—than to negotiate new interaction patterns with people from a variety of cultural backgrounds. Second, such assertiveness engages the ethnic or racial group's intellectual leaders, who have a stake in its perpetuation. If urban schools with a large Puerto Rican component in the student body start offering courses in Puerto Rican poetry, someone has got to teach them, and these teachers then have a stake in their continuation. If a nation splits into two on the basis of ethnicity, two sets of political leaders are established, and each has a stake in the perpetuation of its regime. Third, political leaders find it easy and convenient to appeal to ethnic sentiments in their vote seeking. The large number of political luminaries who turn out for the St. Patrick's Day parade in many northern U.S. cities increases the parade's visibility and the ethnic community's stake in the parade. This is why the issue of a gay Irish group marching in New York City's St. Patrick's Day parade has been so vexed in recent years. On one hand, the parade is privately sponsored, so theoretically the sponsors can invite whomever they want to march; on the other hand, the mayor and other city and state politicians are always prominent, and New York's politicians, especially those from the city, are reluctant to alienate the gay community. The interaction between cultural and political agendas leads to escalation of the conflict. And because ethnic culture is always "colorful," the media treat the dispute to lavish coverage.

The cultural expression of ethnicity is less straightforward than might first appear. Ethnic and racial groups have their subdivisions, often invisible to outsiders, and the question of whose culture gets promoted, gets taken as the culture of the entire group, may be hotly contested. In the United States, many Spanish speakers resent being lumped with one another as "Hispanic," pointing out that Dominicans and Argentineans have little in common. West Indians and African Americans eye one another warily; Koreans fear the economic inroads being made by Thais, while Thais look over their shoulders at Vietnamese. These divisions get played out in local negotiations over multiculturalism. It is all very well to represent different cultures in the curriculum, but how many cultures? Do differences between northern and southern Italians get expressed in the Columbus Day celebration—traditionally associated with Italian ethnicity—and how do the claims of Native Americans get represented in a celebration of the "discoverer" of their lands? Ethnicity itself is a cultural object, with different creators and different recipients, all constructing different meanings. When I'm in Europe, I'm clearly an "American," while in America, I'm variously a "WASP," an "Anglo," a "Yankee," a "white," a "honky," a "Midwesterner." And in Nigeria, I am—along with anyone else having white skin—a "European." My body is a cultural object having ethnic characteristics that different creators use to communicate with different audiences.

Nigeria exemplifies some of the difficulties of ethnic representation. Within this country of some 88 million people are at least 250 distinct languages associated with different ethnic groups (some put the count as high as 400). The three majority languages—Hausa, Yoruba, and Igbo— are spoken by roughly two-thirds of the population. Although no one is happy with English as the lingua franca, none of the three majority linguistic groups wants to give way to another, while the many minority groups fear domination by the "big three" and therefore strongly support the use of English for commercial and governmental transactions. Thus the evening news broadcast by the Nigerian Television Authority is read in English; at the close of the program, the announcer says goodnight in Hausa, Yoruba, and Igbo—much to the disgust of the minority Nigerians, who have strongly protested this bit of symbolism. What seems a low-cost gesture to NTA is an arrogant expression of would-be cultural domination to the Efik, Ibibio, Tiv, and dozens of other minority ethnic groups.

Racial and ethnic affiliations seem natural, matters of blood and bone. But once again, sociologists have pointed out, both are cultural constructs. A person who is one-eighth black is "white" in Jamaica, "black" in Louisiana. Trinidadians and Belizeans, who come from countries a thousand miles apart and regard themselves as having little in common, become ethnically lumped as "West Indians" when they immigrate to Britain, just as the derogatory term "Pakis" is applied by British racists to Hindu Indians, Muslim Pakistanis, and any other South Asians who happen to be around. A "Paki" is not a person, but a cultural object.

Even though people may be lumped together by outsiders or by historical circumstances, they may also take advantage of this imposed ethnicity.

Stephen Cornell (1988) studied how Native Americans came to recognize a shared identity and common political agenda. For Native Americans living on reservations during most of the twentieth century, tribal and subtribal affiliations were the significant markers of identification both to themselves and to others with whom they came into contact. But in the 1950s and 1960s, increasing numbers came to such cities as Los Angeles and Chicago, seeking the economic opportunities that their desolate reservations lacked. Here they clustered in the same down-and-out neighborhoods, dealt with the same bureaucracies, hung out at the same bars, and sometimes were subject to the same prejudices as "dirty Indians" or "red niggers." Now the cultural identity that mattered was not Oglala or Cree but "Indian." This recognition of shared identity led urban Indians to assert common cultural and political claims. One of the most visible and influential fruits of this new supratribalism was the aggressive organization known as A.I.M. (American Indian Movement), which pressed Indian issues in the 1970s.

Cultural expressions of ethnicity, like the African-American holiday of Kwanzaa, designed by a California professor in the late 1960s, are often cases of the "invention of tradition," not of venerable ritual. Ethnicity and race are artificial constructs, the results of historical contingencies. At the same time, they exert enormous motivational influence, instilling fierce loyalties and equally fierce hatreds. Heterogeneous states and social groups (e.g., communities, schools, organizations) are thus obliged to find ways to acknowledge and perhaps celebrate cultural diversity while constructing a common culture, of which the different ethnic or racial groups are subcultures, that successfully claims the primary allegiance of every citizen. This is no simple task, and it is made harder by local habits and prejudices. Many Chinese in Malaysia feel stronger ties to Chinese elsewhere than they do to Muslim Malays, who have severely restricted their opportunities. Some American Jews donate vast amounts of money to Israel, often more than they do to local charities. Some blacks of the African diaspora argue that their primary ties should be to one another, rather than to the nations in which they happen to live (this was the impulse behind the Negritude movement, for example). Against this backdrop of separation, communities, nations, and transnational bodies like the European Union promote the image of a common culture and fate. So far, the claims of ethnicity, resting on what has been termed a "constructed primordialism" (Appadurai, 1990), have remained strong enough to frustrate the cosmopolitans, resulting both in indisputable pride and unspeakable bloodshed.

The Wars of Modernity

Assertions of ethnic and racial particularism are examples of a more general phenomenon: the failure of modernity to realize its goal of enlightened humanism. Ever since the eighteenth-century Enlightenment, Western social thought has regarded the modern era as strikingly different from any that preceded it. Modernity was seen as the stage in social evolution characterized by reason and the rational application of human ingenuity to nature; by popular participation in determining government leaders and policies; by secularization, freedom from superstition and myths; by technological advances, generally involving industrialization; by urbanization; by universal education; and by possible, if not inevitable, victory over disease and want.

The discipline of sociology, furthermore, has been first and foremost the science of modernity. Sociology's founding fathers—Marx, Durkheim, and Weber—all envisioned a modern society in which particular or ascribed characteristics, things we were born with, such as skin color, family name, religion, or region of origin, would matter less and less. They envisioned a society of specialized knowledge, where positions were filled by individual merit, where human freedom was in tension with impersonal bureaucracies, where everything was clear and efficient but possibly soulless as well. Early science fiction gave a popular culture rendering of the sociological brave new world, where deracinated explorers in unisex space suits traveled the universe representing a common humanity.

For good or ill, society, even society in advanced industrial/postindustrial societies, has not experienced the transformations expected by either social science or science fiction. Particularisms of race and ethnicity persist. Religion has not faded away. Traditions, whether genuinely old or invented, have remained compelling. And modernity itself has prompted strong cultural reactions in two directions: postmodernism and fundamentalism.

Postmodernism is the term many people now apply to the culture of contemporary society, just as modernism—abstract art, atonal music, psychoanalysis, stream-of-consciousness fiction, starkly functional architecture, the anomie produced by rapid social change—was the culture of modern society. Many people believe that society has entered this new stage beyond modernity, a postindustrial stage of social development dominated by media images, in which people are connected with other places and other times through proliferating channels of information. If the modern person was characterized by hope and anxiety, the postmodern person is characterized by a cool absence of illusion. Modern minds were skeptical; postmodern minds are cynical.

I return to the subject of postmodernism in Chapter 7. For now, let's consider only one aspect of postmodern culture, what has been called the "decline of metanarrative." This rather clumsy expression refers to the fact that previous eras seemed always to have a story (a narrative) that located and defined them. For the European Middle Ages, for example, the story was Christian history: the Creation, Adam's fall, Christ's life, the period awaiting Christ's return (in which the "present" was invariably located), the Second Coming, the Last Judgment. The modern period produced equivalent secular narratives that featured the drama of social evolution (whereby humanity was evolving, through competition, toward ever more complex and higher forms) or the drama of Marxism (whereby class conflicts moved through a series of economic stages from feudalism to capitalism and, ultimately, communism).

Theorists of postmodernism argue that many people no longer believe in such master-stories of social change. In the place of metanarrative is a growing cynicism based on the sense that life is meaningless and culture only a play of images without reference to some underlying reality. We might conceive of this postmodern model as a version of reflection theory, only with mirrors facing each another instead of the social world. Postmodern cultural objects exhibit freedom and exuberance. Because signifiers need not be connected with any specific meanings, a postmodern building can have Gothic spires, Renaissance arches, modern windows, and a Spanish colonial courtyard; only a fool mired in some metanarrative swamp would try to interpret such a building. At the same time, the movement's self-conscious elevation of meaninglessness—making a virtue out of anomie—can result in an empty nihilism.

Some scholars have maintained that postmodernism is a particular stage and style of modernism, rather than something altogether new. Both modernism and postmodernism, they argue, are the expressive aspects (the culture) of modernity, defined as a society characterized by industrial production, advanced division of labor, international exchanges, and a rationalized life world—which is just what the social scientists and science fiction writers envisioned all along. This modernity, furthermore, with its modern or postmodern cultural objects, has produced an exceedingly strong countermovement, one that appears worldwide. This is the impulse toward religious fundamentalism.

Fundamentalisms appear in many forms—Hindus tearing down the Babri mosque, Shiite Muslims overthrowing the Shah of Iran, American Christians demanding prayer in, and sex education out of, schools. What all such movements have in common is their vehement rejection of modernity, or at least of certain aspects of modernity. Social changes (in Durkheimian terms, the growing realm of the profane) appear to impinge on their most sacred values. Sometimes fundamentalists retreat from "the world," attempting to live according to their own lights, like the Amish in rural America. Others attack. The Hindus who sacked the mosque were protesting four decades of Indian secular democracy, for example, that had seemed to produce plenty of corruption but little economic improvement in most people's lives. They looked for a different vision, and Hindu fundamentalism offered one. Biba Chandra, an Indian political scientist, said, "People see the whole system as corrupt and dysfunctional. . . . The value system of the last 30 years has cracked. As a result, people look for alternatives. They turn back to religion, to caste, to anything that promises them an identity" (Hundley, 1993). Although sociology as a discipline has generally assumed increasing secularization and postmodernists have celebrated it, fundamentalists assert the older claims of religion and traditional social patterns, which they regard as justified by religion. Their single-mindedness and passionate commitment attract many to their cause, for they offer a fixed set of meanings and interpretations, often based on a religious text, that provides stability in a chaotic world. In other words, they offer a culture with clear meanings, and a metanarrative.

Fundamentalism typically has social origins involving rural-to-urban immigration that displace community-based power structures (Arjomad, 1988). For example, Kevin Neuhouser (1989) has shown that in squatters' settlements outside Brazilian cities, women wield far greater power than they did in their rural villages of origin because the men are away from the settlements pursuing or seeking jobs in the urban labor markets; furthermore, women are responsible for organizing vital services such as the water supply, and these organizations sometimes serve as the basis for a broader political organization. Such an unsettling of traditional sex-power relations may lead to new relations or to a renewed assertion of machismo. Fundamentalism is one response to such change. Martin Riesbrodt (1993), who compared Iranian Shiite fundamentalism in the 1970s to American Protestant fundamentalism of the 1920s, contends that both represent the attempt to reassert patriarchal control in the teeth of modern urbanism.

Although religious fundamentalism represents an extreme case, most advanced countries are experiencing what James Davison Hunter (1991) labeled "culture wars" between traditionalists and modernists, those who are uncomfortable with change and those who embrace it. Frequently, these "wars" are over gender roles and sexuality, as in the battles over legalization of contraception in Ireland, the veiling of women in Egypt and much of the Middle East, the clitoridectomy in Africa, or gays in the military in the United States. Sex and gender relations become metaphors for social change. The breakdown of ascriptive positions involves much more struggle than predicted by the discipline of sociology, which also failed to foretell that fundamentalism and traditional culture would in many cases be at least temporarily victorious.

Nowhere is this phenomenon clearer than in the American controversy over abortion. Pro-life activists assert that the traditional set of gender responsibilities—in which men are held responsible for supporting both the children they have fathered and their mothers, and in which women are honored because of their capacity for motherhood—will be overturned if abortion decouples sex from parenthood. Pro-choice activists assert that women's advances, based on the social changes that have brought women greater freedom and opportunity in the public sector, will falter if women lack reproductive freedoms and control over their own bodies. Kristen Luker (1984) sees the roots of the abortion conflict in the different market positions held by educated, career-oriented, pro-choice women on the one hand and less-educated, family-oriented, pro-life women on the other. Anthropologist Faye Ginsberg (1989) believes the differences between the two worldviews are less ones of socioeconomic position and more ones of different formative experiences. For pro-choice women, early exposure to unconventional female role models—strong women active outside the realm of motherhood—seems key to their commitment to women being able to make their own decisions regarding pregnancy and abortion; for pro-life women, having a baby often prompts a spiritual conversion to a strong stand against abortion. Regardless of its source, in the battle over abortion both sides pursue their legal objectives by cultural means, specifically by attempting to control meanings. Their rhetoric makes this clear; one side speaks of abortion as "terminating a pregnancy," the other as "killing a baby."

Local skirmishes in this ongoing conflict likewise involve producing and creating meaningful cultural objects for a local audience. Ginsberg (1989) described how an abortion clinic in Fargo, North Dakota, quietly began its operations in a restored old house; its staff and their pro-choice supporters tried to have the clinic "mean" business as usual, nothing remarkable. But moderate pro-life groups set up vigils in front of the clinic in which pairs of women walked back and forth holding Bibles and praying; they tried to make the clinic "mean" that something sinful was happening inside, something that required prayer to combat. Later, less moderate pro-life groups came with placards and handout photos of mutilated babies; shouting at women entering the clinic, and effectively drawing media attention, they tried to make the clinic mean "On this field the forces of good and evil are locked in mortal combat." Once again, we see recipients of a cultural object, conditioned by different horizons of expectations, attributing different meanings to that object and, at the same time, attempting to produce new meanings for different audiences.

Summary

Most people regard social problems as malfunctions in the social system, and as such the problems demand solutions. A social problem may be complex; apparent problems may be symptomatic of larger, underlying problems; entrenched economic or political interests may stand in the way. But all problems, we believe, have solutions if only enough resources, ingenuity, and moral courage are brought to bear on them.

Thinking of social problems less as givens and more as cultural objects draws attention to the artificial construction of any one problem and to the implied meanings that are conveyed when a problem gets defined in one way and not another. Very different interests are engaged in constructing a particular problem as "homosexuality," or as "sex outside marriage," or as "a highly contagious virus spread by bodily fluids," and very different lines of action—different solutions—are implied. This is not to suggest that social problems, however defined, have no relation to human suffering. People do sicken and die of AIDS, no matter what cultural object is being constructed as "the problem." Applying a cultural diamond analysis to a social problem does suggest, however, that such problems, like all cultural objects, have specific creators and recipients. They also have careers; like any cultural object, a social problem can rise in popularity, can become institutionalized, or can fail to win an audience and disappear. Understanding this allows us to construct other formulations of a problem and to imagine solutions.

In this chapter, we have seen how social problems involving economic inequality, ethnicity, and modernity itself are cultural constructions, rather than natural events or random happenings. One may apply a cultural diamond analysis to virtually any social problem. If we set up the cultural object to be, for example, (1) "illegal drugs entering America and threatening its citizens," we are appealing to an audience of Americans fearful of attacks on their way of life. We are invoking images of contamination from foreign sources. We are implying solutions: declaring a national "war" on drugs, strengthening the national defense against penetration by drugs, taking military action against the foreign producers. It is not surprising that the creators of this cultural object are the federal government (most recently the Bush administration, although administrations from both parties have waged war on drugs). Cultural creators create problems for which they have solutions, and governments know how to wage war. If the drug problem were defined differently, so that the cultural object was (2) "poverty and despair that prompt a narcotic-induced withdrawal from reality," then the solution would not be war, but relieving poverty and despair, something that governments are less successful at doing. It is not surprising that academics and armchair social critics construct this second cultural object more often than politicians and government administrators do, for professors and critics are not responsible for providing the solutions. There are many other ways to construct the cultural object of drugs-as-social-problem. We could call the problem "sin," or "laws attempting to regulate private behavior," or "poor individual decision making," or "wicked drug dealers." Different cultural creators, a different intended audience, different meanings and solutions exist for each such cultural object.

All cultural objects are not equal, however, for different ones will be able to mobilize different resources. Calling a "war on" anything enables the government to take action, whereas constructing the same thing as "sin" precludes government action. As a practical matter, the best cultural object for embodying a social problem is one that (1) unambiguously isolates happenings and turns them into events relevant to the cultural object, (2) captures the attention of a larger or powerful set of recipients, and (3) suggests solutions that are within the capacity of the relevant institutions. Thus "segregation" is a well-formed social problem for the government to construct as a cultural object because it meets all three criteria, while "racial hatred" is not, for it is diffused among various happenings and its solutions are beyond government capacities. On the other hand, the parents of a family can tackle the problem of racial hatred among its members but can do little about segregation.

A cultural object, as we have seen, is an interpretation, a set of meanings that fit a context of ideas and institutions, that translate random happenings into events, and that suggest attitudes and actions. Social problems are cultural objects in exactly this sense. Tracing the links among the problems, their creators, their receivers, and their social worlds will help illuminate those solutions that might work, those that probably will not, and those that have not yet been imagined because of how the problem has been constructed.

RECOMMENDED FOR FURTHER READING

Gusfield, Joseph R. 1981. *The Culture of Public Problems: Drinking-Driving and the Symbolic Order.* Chicago: University of Chicago Press. Using interactionism and dramaturgical analysis, Gusfield shows why the "killer drunk" has captured the popular imagination as the key to the social problem of auto fatalities.

Hilgartner, Stephen and Bosk, Charles L. 1988. "The Rise and Fall of Social Problems: A Public Arenas Model." *American Journal of Sociology* 94: 53-78. Drawing on a wide variety of social problems, the authors sketch a model of how problems compete with each other for public attention.

Willis, Paul. (1977) 1981. *Learning to Labor: How Working Class Kids Get Working Class Jobs.* New York: Columbia University Press. From extensive participant observation in a working-class high school, Willis gives a detailed ethnographic study of the official and the subversive cultures through which the students make their lives meaningful.

6

Culture and Organizations:
Getting Things Done
in a Multicultural World

People who work for organizations think of themselves as practical types,
looking to get the job done, improve the bottom line, implement the policy.
Yet just like those who tackle social problems, organization men and women
often find themselves dealing with the expressive and the symbolic—
with culture. Many of the ambiguities of organizational life derive from
the role that culture and cultural objects play, both within the organization and impinging on its operations from outside. In this chapter, we
explore how culture affects the ways people conduct business transactions, how governments try to implement programs, and organizations
try to produce and market products—like hamburgers, for instance.

The man who holds the Israeli franchise for McDonald's wrestles with
a big problem: reconciling his business objectives with Israel's religious
laws and sensibilities (Haberman, 1993). Israelis adore American popular
culture, and nothing is more emblematic of all things American than a
Big Mac. Nothing is less kosher, either, and therein lies the problem. Should
the franchiser simply write off that portion of his potential market that
demands kosher food, thereby eliminating a significant bloc of consumers before the first Israeli McDonald's ever opens its doors? Should he try
to make kosher burgers, a strategy pursued by several other chains that
was not particularly successful?

Two aspects of Israeli culture seem relevant here. The first is the role
of religion in daily life. On the one hand, most Israelis are Jews who do
not actively practice their religion. Israel has many thriving nonkosher
restaurants, and the stratum most likely to patronize McDonald's, the
young and with-it, are the least likely to be religiously observant. On the
other hand, Orthodox Jews act as a cultural watchdog, ready to pounce
on anything that seems too blatantly disrespectful of religious doctrines.
For example, Pepsi-Cola's Israeli producer ran an advertising campaign

showing the human race evolving from the apes and reaching its highest stage of evolution clutching a Pepsi. Orthodox rabbis objected, not to the sheer silliness of the ad, but to the fact that the evolutionary theme violated the biblical story of the Creation. When the rabbis threatened to withdraw the soda's kosher certification, the Pepsi producer withdrew the ads. In spite of the secularism of most of his market, he learned that offending the observant was bad business.

The second cultural factor has to do with how Israelis, especially young Israelis, feel about American pop culture. They not only embrace it, but they also have a sophisticated appreciation of its finer details. A pseudo-Big Mac that was "religiously correct" would be spotted at once and, in all likelihood, despised. As one Israeli newspaper put it, "A strictly kosher hamburger could not meet the culinary demands of the experts. The Israeli continued to dream about real hamburgers. Each time he went abroad, he lunged at the first hamburger joint in sight" (Haberman, 1993). So compromise might be bad business, too.

The Israeli businessman's dilemma typifies a common theme: reconciling global and local cultures. Global culture, strongly influenced by American popular culture and spread by the media and travelers, makes the Big Mac available as a culture object, as shown in Figure 6-1. In this case, the cultural object is created indirectly by an American corporation and directly by an Israeli franchiser attempting to reach those Israeli consumers who accept the corporation's promotion of a certain set of associations. In its global construction, the burger as cultural object means (Meaning #1) up-to-date, American, fresh, youthful, trendy. But locally, the Big Mac and other McDonald's fare are cultural objects, too. As constructed by religious conservatives, they are (Meaning #2) nonkosher, non-Jewish, alien, assimilationist, an affront to religion and Jewish identity. The businessman wants to capitalize on the first set of meanings and reach the audience with whom it resonates. He wants to isolate the second set—he knows an orthodox Jew is never going to chow down on a Quarter Pounder with cheese anyway—and keep it from influencing a larger audience. Ideally, he would like to deconstruct this second cultural object altogether so that McDonald's does not mean alien or non-Jewish, even though it does mean American and global-trendy. As part of his business planning, he is preparing a survey to see just how, as a practical matter, secular Israeli Jews think about kosher. Does their working definition of kosher rule out all cheeseburgers or just those topped with bacon?

Making profits, doing business generally, getting results—these activities are more complicated in a global economy where local and international cultures clash, where incompatible meaning systems must be

Figure 6-1

McDonald's in Israel

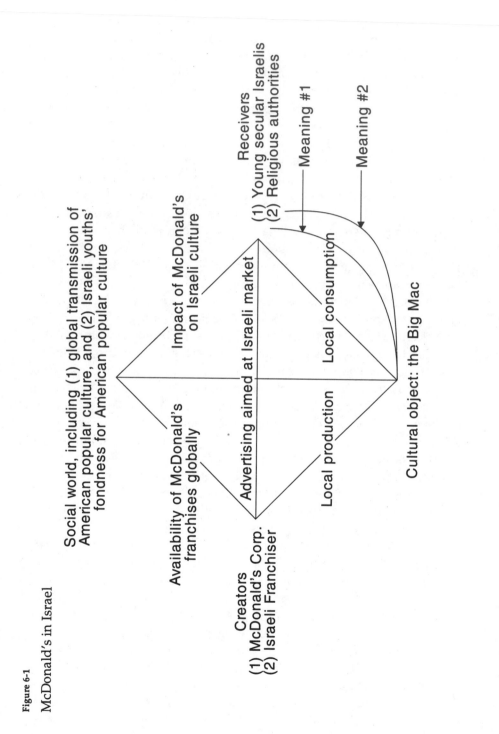

reconciled, where the people doing business or working for an organization cannot avoid managing meanings just as much as they manage money,
products, and people. In this chapter we explore four ways in which culture
affects the ways organizations accomplish their objectives, or fail to, in a
rapidly changing world. We begin by considering organizational cultures, first at the individual level, examining the relationship between
culture and motivation; then we consider the cultures that can emerge at
different levels of employees within organizations. Next, we look at some
research on the way in which national cultures shape organizational
outcomes. And finally, we explore the problems of those organizations
and programs that must operate across a multiplicity of cultures.

Organizational Cultures

Organizations operate within and across cultures, but they also produce
cultures of their own. Managers and workers create and receive cultural
objects—shared meanings embodied in forms—that may facilitate or
obstruct the organization's operations. We can think of this exchange of
meanings as operating at two levels: the individual or small group level,
and the level of the larger group ("the workers") or even the organization
as a whole. Let us first consider the micro-level, where group subcultures
arise to create a meaningful working world.

Culture and Motivation

How does a leader or a manager get people to work hard, cooperate,
extend themselves for the good of the whole, or do anything they wouldn't
otherwise do? This is a standard problem faced by the management of
every organization, whether a corner grocery, a religious sect, a government
agency, or a transnational corporation. The most direct way to motivate
compliance is through the exercise of force: Most people will respond
most of the time if they are threatened with a whip or a gun. But raw power
is inefficient, not to mention inhumane. Prison labor or slave systems are
seldom cost effective in the long run, nor are they options for most contemporary organizations. So how do managers motivate people to work?

One theory is based on the idea of economic man, which goes like this:
Human beings want money and the things money will buy. Because their
wants and desires are always greater than their means, they will work more
for more pay. This theory is the basis for wage payment systems such as
piecework, whereby a worker's pay is a direct function of his output. In

such a system, a company may calculate that the average worker can turn out nine widgets per hour, and the standard pay is pegged to this output. If a worker exceeds the established standard of production—in other words, if he makes ten widgets an hour when the standard is nine —he gets a bonus. If he only turns out six widgets, on the other hand, his earnings may get docked.

As plausible as it sounds, the economic incentive theory often doesn't seem to work. Studies of work units have repeatedly shown that a group will establish a reasonable rate of production, one that its members can achieve without much difficulty, and most individuals in the group will not exceed it (Homans, 1950). Those who produce more are derisively called "rate busters," just as overachievers in school are sometimes scorned as "teacher's pets." The social pressure exerted by the group will usually bring the rate busters into line. Similarly, those who fall behind will be helped by other group members even though it is not in the latter's economic interest to do so.

We have seen this phenomenon before: the creation of a subculture, with its own meanings and practices, that buffers its members from external influences. The same thing that happens in Little League teams and among pot smokers also happens in government bureaucracies and business firms. As with those examples, we can reinterpret organizational subcultures in terms of the cultural diamond. What the external culture creates as a cultural object—an incentive system wherein extra effort "means" more pay—is received by subculture members who have a distinctively different horizon of expectations. For them, the piecework system "means" inequalities within the group that make everyone's life more difficult and that, perhaps, encourage management to raise the standard level of expected production. So the group creates its own cultural object, an amount of output that "means" a reasonable level of production and group harmony. But the managerial audience for such an output level sees it as indicating workers' recalcitrance and inability to perceive their own economic interests.

Saleswomen in department stores of the early twentieth century, for example, set up their own "counter cultures," whereby they ignored the management incentive system in favor of a "stint," an amount of sales they judged to be a fair day's work (Benson, 1986). Each worker monitored her sales, and as she approached her day's stint, she would slacken her selling efforts, perhaps by doing some stock work off the selling floor. Those who had already made their stint for the day would steer sales to those who were behind. Eager beavers who ignored the stint and tried to generate too many sales were labeled "grabbers" and risked social isolation from the department's subculture unless they changed their ways.

Similar accounts of the subversion of managerial objectives by small-group worker cultures occur worldwide. When American firms open operations in other countries, for instance, they often have a problem with nepotism or other forms of particular favoritism. To the American executives, individual employees should be judged and treated on their own merits; showing favoritism is a form of corruption. But to the local employees, favoring someone from your home village (in China), your family (in Italy), or your ethnic group (in Nigeria) by promoting that person over others who are equally qualified means expressing appropriate group solidarity. Similarly, what looks like a bribe to Westerners looks like a legitimate monetary show of respect and gratitude, perhaps delivered before the fact, to many people in developing countries.

If neither sheer economic incentives nor the forceful imposition of bureaucratic rules can be counted on to motivate desired behavior in workers, then, what does work? Organizations have tried a variety of approaches, all involving the attempt to create a certain type of organizational culture in which hard work and commitment to the goals of the organization are part of a meaningful complex of activities and attitudes. Some organizations have applied structural solutions to the problem of bureaucratic alienation—for example, by having few hierarchical steps and by locating decision making at relatively low levels (cf. Burns & Stalker, 1961). Instead of a tall, thin organizational chart, these firms have a short, fat one; they typically stress informality and accessibility, encourage innovation, and avoid such status markers as executive cafeterias. The closer the average employees are to the centers of decision and control, managerial reasoning runs, the greater influence they have over outcomes, and the less social distance there is between top management and everyone else, the more "everyone else" will identify with and contribute to achieving the goals of the organization.

A second way of ensuring that employees share the goals of the organization is to foster a preferred type of organizational culture directly by selectivity at the recruitment stage and by active socialization. This strategy is perhaps most notable among Japanese organizations. With sufficient selectivity and intense socialization, even high employee turnover may not disturb the organizational culture (Harrison & Carroll, 1991). In her study of flight attendants, Arlie Hochschild analyzed how airlines promote an organizational culture of caring for customers by (1) selecting flight attendants who are naturally sympathetic, extroverted people and (2) training them to have the proper emotional responses, including feeling genuine concern for the passengers' comfort and genuine satisfaction when a passenger is happy. Hochschild calls this "emotion labor," or the selling of feelings for wages, and she regards it as a little- noticed form of gender discrimination (the airlines and the passengers expect more emotion labor from women than from men). The point here, however, is not whether or not the airlines' recruitment and training are exploitative, but simply their success in instilling an organizational culture among their employees.

Structural and cultural attempts to motivate organizational commit-ment often go hand in hand. Typical of this combination is a high-tech engineering company studied by Gideon Kunda (1992). The firm's organi-zational structure, all parties agree, is decentralized, vague, and con-stantly changing. This ambiguous structure is compatible with the firm's strong and oft-asserted culture of self-management (lines of authority aren't important), joint decision making (specified positional responsi-bilities are beside the point), and profit-oriented creativity (which a heavy-handed bureaucratic structure might stifle). "Tech culture," repeatedly instilled through both organizational rituals and everyday routines, pro-duces employee commitment through normative control, which is an organizational "attempt to elicit and direct the required efforts of mem-bers by controlling the underlying experiences, thoughts, and feelings that guide their actions" (p. 11). Normative control, in other words, is what any social group's dominant culture is usually about. This company's managers happen to be exceptionally aware of this fact and thus promote an organizational culture to serve the firm's interests.

A third way managers motivate employees is by setting up models of thought and behavior in the form of exemplary actors and organizational stories. Model actors, like Lowenthal's "heroes of production," are both personally honored and presented as worthy of emulation. Hospital walls may display pictures of the "employee of the month," for example, just as real estate firms publicly honor those agents with the highest sales. The functions of honoring the exceptional and rewarding the faithful may contradict each other at times; in a grocery story where there are always several "employees of the week," the honor is devalued and its motiva-tional capacity diminished because of its ubiquity. If it is not overdone, however, the model actor becomes a cultural object, simultaneously a model of good behavior and a model for other members of the organiza-tion (Geertz, 1973).

The Chinese government has made conspicuous use of exemplary models. In 1963, Lin Biao, chosen by Mao to head the People's Liberation Army, initiated a campaign to remind the PLA's soldiers that their first obligation was service to the Chinese Communist Party (Spence, 1990). The campaign centered on the *Diary of Lei Feng*, a posthumously discovered journal in which a young soldier recorded his loyalty to the CCP, to Chairman Mao, and to his duty. Lei Feng was an army truck driver whose peasant family had suffered cruelly under the pre-Revolutionary landlords. Lei Feng's army career exemplified faithful service and sacrifice; he once declared, "I will be a screw that never rusts and will glitter anywhere I am placed." He died as he had lived, run over by a truck while he was helping a comrade. The diary became required reading in Chinese schools, promoted by Mao himself as a model of how the entire nation should "learn from the PLA." In reality, this model actor was a fiction. The fact that Lei Feng's diary had been concocted by the propaganda wing of the PLA did not seem to detract from its exemplary power, however, even if some Chinese suspected the truth. As late as 1987, as the CCP grew increasingly resistant to the pro-democracy movement, the party launched a new campaign honoring the "Lei Feng spirit."

Exemplary actors are one type of model; another comes from organizational stories. In orientation and training sessions, managers tell anecdotes that illustrate desired organizational values and practices. A well-known case in the sociology of organizations literature is that retold by Chester Barnard (1939) about the telephone operator who stayed at her switchboard even though she knew her mother was trapped in a burning house; Barnard, a former telephone company executive, hastened to point out that the mother survived. Such stories, managers assume, instill organizational loyalty and motivate desired behavior. But as we have seen in our discussion of worker subcultures, another type of story can emerge from interactions among the workers themselves, over and above the accounts sanctioned by management. We need to take a closer look now at how employees make their organizational lives meaningful.

Cultures of Solidarity and Ambiguity

Joanne Martin and colleagues (1983) identified seven types of narratives that appear in a wide variety of public and private organizations. These are stories about breaking rules, the humanity (or lack thereof) of the boss, low-level employees who rise to the top, firing, moving, mistakes made by employees, and the organization's capacity for dealing with obstacles. Martin points out that people who tell these stories understand them as demonstrating the uniqueness of their organization, despite the fact that the identical stories show up in different organizations belying that uniqueness.

Each type of organizational narrative has positive and negative versions. The positive mistake story, for example, has an employee confessing to error and his boss sharing the responsibility with him, while the negative version features an unforgiving boss who never lets the employee off the hook. Martin suggests that common stories express the contradictions and dualities inherent in organizational life; thus, "How will the boss react to mistakes?" stories deal with the duality between security (all employees want job security) and insecurity (organizations must retain the capacity to threaten their employees' security). Expressing such tensions—making collective representations of the facts of organizational life, to return to the Durkheimian language used earlier—may serve to alleviate them. The positive versions of these stories, which are promulgated through organizational histories and rituals, may motivate employees by assuring them that their organization is unique in some way—uniquely benevolent, uniquely open to advancement—even though the ubiquity of such stories suggests that it is not. Even in their negative versions, such stories, as cultural objects, forge solidarity among those who share them.

Having raised the issue of solidarity within organizations, we have moved to a different type of organizational culture, one that emerges, rather than one that is constructed more or less intentionally. Groups of people who work (or play) together produce their own subcultures or idiocultures, but this kind of cultural creation through interaction is not entirely independent of the larger social context. In other words, we must not forget the link on our cultural diamond between the social world and the creators of some cultural objects. For example, even though race, ethnicity, or gender may not "matter" in performing a certain type of job, and although all such categories may be represented in a certain office or factory unit, these characteristics matter powerfully to the outside world. Moreover, members of these groups bring bits and pieces of different cultures with them to work; the Puerto Ricans, on average, have knowledge of common friends, relatives, and institutions that the Mexican Americans don't share. For this reason, worker subcultures may break down along ethnic or gender lines. Management tries to discourage this form of partition because it works against functional equivalence; from a boss's point of view, a trained female African American should be the same as a trained male Samoan, and either one should be capable of task assignments without regard to ascribed characteristics. Cultural affinities are strongly felt, however, and people are drawn to other people who share their meaning systems.

Perhaps the most influential division that affects the emergence of subgroups is that between labor and management. Here most firms and organizations draw clear distinctions, as with soldiers and officers in the army. Usually there are a few intermediate or bridging positions, such as the noncommissioned officers or foremen in a plant, and these positions may be unusually stressful because of divided loyalties; incumbents have often "risen from the ranks," yet no longer share solidarity with those whom they now supervise. The placement of most members of an organization, however, is unambiguous. Symbolism reinforces the divide: the officer's club, the executive cafeteria, the faculty lounge. Practical distinctions abound as well; workers are paid an hourly wage and management earns a monthly salary, for example, or workers are often unionized and managers rarely are.

How does the labor/management divide affect subcultures within an organization? On the one hand, the sharp class consciousness that Marx envisioned does not seem to apply in many places. In the United States, most working people view themselves as "middle class" regardless of their position, whereas in China a similarly placed person might well define himself as "a worker" or one of "the people." In a homogeneous society such as Japan, company unions and worker-manager socializing bridges the gap, whereas in a heterogeneous society such as Nigeria, ethnicity both bridges the gap and works against solidarity at either the labor or management level.

Because Marxian class consciousness seems to represent a nineteenth-century European model that has grown less relevant over time, some sociologists have concluded that class solidarities themselves are irrelevant to organizational analysis. In American firms, so the argument goes, workers are individualistic, seeking their own personal advancement and comfort. Subgroups may emerge to curb and channel individualism, but they are neither class based nor devoted to pursuing class interests. In his study of instances where worker solidarity did emerge in American firms, Rick Fantasia (1988) showed that class consciousness is neither irrelevant nor unproblematically given, but instead is a cognitive frame that emerges during certain labor/management struggles. "Cultures of solidarity" arise in times of organizational crisis, such as a strike or layoff, when systems of meaning and action among the workers oppose the dominant regime within the organization. Not synonymous with unions, "cultures of solidarity are more or less bounded groupings that may or may not develop a clear organizational identity and structure, but represent the active expression of worker solidarity within an industrial system and a society hostile to it" (p. 19). Although a high level of class consciousness is not always present, conflict and consciousness do emerge under certain specific conditions within an organization, and the workers' solidarities that result are likely to persist well after the conflict that initiated them.

Fantasia analyzed three emerging cultures of solidarity. One of his cases was the mobilization and collective action carried out by nurses and other women workers in a Vermont hospital. For a decade and more, nurses had labored under a contradiction: The greater need for them to acquire specialized technical skills had been offset by cost-cutting measures that appeared to denigrate these skills. The nurses experienced simultaneous professionalization and proletarianization, and many felt that the demand for greater technical skill, coupled with the demand that they care for an increasing number of patients, resulted in their inability to do their jobs properly. Other employees, such as housekeeping and cafeteria workers, were disgruntled over low pay levels and blocked opportunities. Conditions were ripe for unionization. Ironically, management recognized this fact and sought to ward off labor organization through a worker/management policy advisory committee. When a new hospital administrator, concerned that the committee was developing into a collective bargaining vehicle, abolished it, the workers were affronted, and the idea of some form of collective representation in opposition to the administration became firmly planted. In this promising context, representatives of the National Union of Hospital and Health Care Employees began working to organize the hospital in 1981.

The following months saw a series of actions and reactions as management and workers responded to one another with hardening lines of division and, at least on the workers' part, a growing solidarity that fed on its own successes and failures. Management initiated "one-on-ones" in which supervisors attempted to dissuade undecided workers from supporting the union; pro-union workers responded by intruding on these conferences, thereby modifying the impact of the confrontation with authority. Union supporters tried to exhort fellow workers to join their side; management responded by keeping a close eye on pro-union leaders and preventing them from holding union-related discussions on the job. In such an atmosphere, class consciousness did indeed emerge and permeated not only the hospital (in the final election, the union was voted in) but also the homes of many workers, where traditional sexual divisions of labor often had to be modified in light of the long hours required by the wife's organizing activities. Husbands who were themselves union members proved especially supportive because they shared a common set of meanings with their wives.

Research like Fantasia's shows how a workers' culture can emerge. But what about a managerial culture? Do the upper echelons of an organization simply represent the dominant national culture, or is there a distinct culture of managers and owners representing the elite, the bourgeoisie? Max Weber suggested "both of the above." Attitudes toward the link between hard work and worldly success (the latter being a token of heavenly success) persisted long after their basis in religious belief had atrophied. Because these attitudes were held by the dominant middle class—and had, in fact, assisted in its rise—they tended toward cultural domination, as a perusal of nineteenth-century schoolbooks with their penny-saved-is-a-penny-earned maxims made clear. Until well into the twentieth century, the link between hard work and success, and between the success of a firm and the prosperity of the social order ("What's good for General Motors is good for the U.S.A."), was confidently upheld by the business class and was little questioned by everyone else.

No one believes in these links anymore, least of all managers in business, contends Robert Jackall (1988). Instead, managers attempt to negotiate their way through "moral mazes" where success is more a function of propitious alliances and avoiding blame than hard work or productivity, and where managers take their ethical bearings not from an internal moral code, but from what their boss wants and what influences seem to be currently ascendant—"looking up and looking around," Jackall calls it. In the upper levels of corporate culture, a bureaucratic ethic has replaced Weber's Protestant ethic, with the result that a firm's contribution to social welfare is a public relations problem. This managerial subculture upholds an increasing abstraction of organizational functions and a "psychic asceticism" whereby the manager's rationalized self becomes a tool for advancement in his work life that is increasingly removed from home or extra-work relationships. A memorable example occurs in Joseph Heller's novel *Something Happened*, in which we are given a complete description of the bureaucratic politics in which the manager-protagonist is immersed, while the product his organization makes is never mentioned once.

So far we have looked at two models of organizational culture, one emphasizing consensus, the other cleavage. In the *consensus model*, shared goals and values within an organization are the norm and dissidence is a problem requiring correction. This model, which assumes a single organizational culture, is essentially functionalist. In the *cleavage model*, groups within an organization have different interests; the classic fault line falls between labor and management, but gender, ethnicity, or organizational location (e.g., engineering vs. marketing) can give rise to comparable cultures of solidarity. These differing interests predictably generate intraorganization conflict. The cleavage model, rooted in Marxism and other conflict sociologies, sees apparent consensus as a problem because it constitutes the subordination of group interests under the dominant ideology of the capitalist class.

Joanne Martin (1992) has pointed out a third model, one she labels "fragmentation," that questions both the harmony of the consensus model ("integration," in Martin's terms) and the stability and predictability of the cleavage model ("differentiation"). In the fragmentation model, organizations are riddled with ambiguity and people hold multiple perspectives. A single person in an organization is not so much an organizational actor (an IBM man) or a member of a salient group (an engineer) as he is a node of intersection of various groups, categories, and affinities (a male Korean American Presbyterian engineer who works for IBM, has a large family, and is politically liberal). Successive issues will activate different identities. A dispute over a new product introduction may find him allied with other engineers, all advocating moving slowly and getting all of the technological bugs worked out, against the marketing department's eagerness to get the product into the field; on the question of company-provided child care, on the other hand, he may be oriented according to his family interests and liberal leanings; and if IBM suddenly loses market share, he may hunker down as a loyal company man and accept a freeze in pay. This being the case, the organizational analyst, rather than looking for a single organizational culture or for conflicting subcultures, should look for the types of issues that call up different meaning systems. Indeed, Martin urges the analyst to adopt all three perspectives, at least provisionally, for a richer understanding of how cultural processes—people making meanings—influence organizational outcomes.

Organizations in Cultural Contexts

We have been looking at internal organizational cultures—from the walls in, so to speak. Now let's look from the walls out. What is the relationship between an organization—a business firm, a school, a government bureaucracy—and the cultural context in which it operates?

In this area of research, the oscillating emphasis between culture and structure parallels the pattern we have seen before. Sociological theories of bureaucracy, especially that of Max Weber, posited that organizations in modern societies converge toward a single highly efficient model: a rationalized bureaucratic structure of positions having clear lines of authority, functional specialization, and a separation of the personal from the bureaucratic. In other words, from an employee's point of view, you know who your boss is, you know what your job is, and your private life is separate from your work life (e.g., you don't own your desk). This is the structure represented by the typical organizational chart of a firm or a government bureau (Weber himself used the Prussian army as his model).

During the 1950s and 1960s, people who studied organizations became increasingly impressed with the variations in this bureaucratic pattern from place to place. Accounting for such differences produced what we might call "national character" accounts, which had as their premise that different societies produced systematic deviations from the Weberian model even though such distinctive bureaucratic forms might impede organizational efficiency. Convergence toward a rationalized bureaucratic norm, what Weber referred to as the "iron cage," was not about to happen across cultures. In a classic study of this type, French sociologist Michel Crozier (1964) revealed that firms in his country proliferated formal rules and exquisite functional distinctions of the "tightening-that-screw-is not in-my-job-description" sort—a bureaucratic inflexibility that was often at odds with the organizational goal of getting the job done. Crozier argued that French culture was highly individualistic and that the French had an aversion to personal dependency relations on the job. Thus, the excessive rules and rigidities, although bureaucratically irrational, were culturally rational in minimizing managerial discretion and employee dependency. In other words, French culture valued autonomy over productivity, and French organizations reflected this value.

Such national culture studies never entirely went out of fashion, in part, because Americans and Europeans continued to be fascinated by Japanese forms of business organization, so different and so infuriatingly successful. But the emphasis on structural analysis that generally prevailed from the late 1960s through the early 1980s combined with a certain unease over national culture models, which seemed both to imply that less developed societies suffered from an inferior culture and to import Eurocentric assumptions where they didn't belong. Even though this line of research did not die out, for some time it was dormant.

By the mid-1980s, the interest in the relationship between organizations and their surrounding cultures came roaring back. The globalization of the economy was the principle reason for this development. Many companies that had formerly been exclusively American or European extended their reach globally, with respect to finance, production, and/or markets. This rapid expansion across national boundaries meant that individual firms, some for the first time, were concerned with understanding cultural differences. The continued success of Japan now was joined with the aggressive "Four Little Dragons" (Taiwan, South Korea, Singapore, and Hong Kong) and new players such as Mexico and Brazil in reshaping the global economy and the way Westerners conceived it. Finally, new theoretical moves within the social sciences were bridging the culture-structure gap, rendering work that explored their mutual influence both plausible and even fashionable.

James Lincoln and Arne Kalleberg's research (1990) offers a good example of the new interest in the interaction of structure and culture to produce organizational outcomes. They began by observing that American business managers and scholars, intrigued by the success of Japanese management techniques, continue to wonder which of these techniques might be successfully imported. From surveys of matched firms in the U.S. and Japan, Lincoln and Kalleberg set out to compare structural versus cultural explanations for differences in worker commitment to firms and in job satisfaction. They labeled as "structural theory" the view that welfare corporatism, widely practiced by Japanese firms, accounts for difference in commitment and job satisfaction; welfare corporatism entailed job security, labor-management cooperation, decentralized decision making with a high degree of worker participation, and corporate sponsorship of employee welfare benefits and social activities. What they called "cultural theory," on the other hand, suggested that national differences in workers' values accounted for national differences in commitment and job satisfaction. The structuralist position implies that welfare corporatism increases worker commitment and satisfaction whenever it is applied; Japanese firms, especially those of the core industries, tend to have more of it, but the same principles would be beneficial anywhere. A strictly "culturalist" (their term) approach, on the other hand, would maintain that the Japanese organizational forms were suited to Japanese culture, which valued the collectivity over the individual, cooperation, and a dependent personal relationship between employees and supervisors (the exact opposite of French values, according to Crozier); according to this view, these forms would not be as successful if exported to other cultures.

Meticulous comparisons both supported the general thrust of the welfare corporatist hypothesis, which the authors initially favored, and suggested persistent cultural differences. As expected, work commitment was higher among the Japanese workers than among the Americans, but—surprisingly—actual job satisfaction was lower. As expected, the quality of the relationships between workers and their co-workers and supervisors was positively associated with commitment and satisfaction, but friendships had no bearing on these outcomes. (Quality of the relationship was measured by such questions as, "How satisfied are you with you supervisor?" while friendship was measured by such questions as, "How often do you get together with your supervisor outside of work?") In the United States, this finding was not surprising—outside get-togethers are not regarded as having much bearing on organizational commitment, but instead are considered to be matters of personal choice. Japan, however, is noted for company social functions and the common pattern in which supervisors and employees go out drinking or to a restaurant, all of which the company sponsors and encourages. Although we might assume that such activities are assiduously cultivated by the Japanese firms because they bind the employees to the organization, such is not the case. It appears that expectations are different; Japanese worker-manager social contacts are routine and therefore are regarded as no big deal, while American workers and managers socialize within their own groups but not with each other (so worker get-togethers could be occasions for bitching about the boss!). In neither culture is the presence or absence of such friendships seen as affecting life on the job.

More generally, the two countries show distinct differences in work values. The Japanese favor close relations with supervisors, working in groups, and a variety of reciprocal ties; the Americans prefer independence in all of these areas. These differences do affect work attitudes, but they do not mediate the effect of the job variables associated with the welfare corporatist hypothesis; such things as employee participation in decision making raise commitment independent of worker values. In other words, although distinct cultural differences affect workers' relations to the firm, at the same time the participatory style of welfare corporatism can produce benefits of commitment and satisfaction in any cultural setting. Once again we see that posing the culture versus structure explanation in either/or terms belies the complexities of real social life.

A promising approach that addresses the interpenetration of culture and structure is known as the new institutionalism (Powell & DiMaggio, 1992). New institutionalist thinking regards organizations not as tightly integrated bureaucracies mobilized to pursue certain goals, but as loosely connected assemblages of people, structures, and systems (Meyer & Rowan, 1977). Moreover, instead of being organized according to a single, rational efficiency principle, organizations and their subunits tend to conform to their institutional contexts. For example, American schools engage in certain symbolic rituals such as the preparation of report cards (cultural objects) because, although learning and educational progress are notoriously hard to measure, the institutional context in which schools find themselves expects organizations to show a bottom line. Report cards or an emphasis on test scores are ways that the school establishes "institutional isomorphism" with its context; making up the report card represents a "ritual of good faith" prepared for the external audience (of parents, school boards, politicians) and is a way of turning aside a more critical inspection of what might really be going on in the school.

Given a certain plasticity of structure, organizations and organizational relationships match and mirror their institutional contexts. This may be particularly true of such organizations as school and government bureaucracies, for which there is no clear "bottom line," but it applies to business firms as well. Moreover, cross-cultural organizational comparisons can readily benefit from a new institutionalist approach. A team of organizational sociologists (Orrù, Biggart, & Hamilton, 1991) compared the structures of business enterprise groups (stable aggregates of firms related by shared ownership or management, mutual financial transactions, and/or other forms of interdependency) in Japan and two of the "Little Dragons"—Taiwan and South Korea. All three countries featured stable enterprise groups having no exact counterparts in the United States. But the structures of enterprise groups differ among the three countries. Japan's groups involve stable, noncompeting horizontal links, "a community of equals" intersected by some vertical, hierarchical links. South Korea, in contrast, has fewer horizontal links; its enterprise groups are centralized outgrowths of a founding patriarch's firm and exhibit "vertical domination." Taiwan is different still; its enterprise groups are small, less central, and both controlled and financed by single families. These different organizational patterns, the authors contended, are isomorphic with other enterprise groups and other institutions within the same society. They represent different cultural principals—that of communitarianism in Japan, patrimonialism in South Korea, and familialism in Taiwan—that are manifest in a variety of institutional settings. This kind of comparison suggests how new institutionalist thinking can reveal connections between national or local culture on the one hand and organizational structure on the other.

Working Across Cultures

It is one thing to recognize that cultural differences have some effect on "getting it done" and that planners or business managers must employ different organizational forms and incentives in Accra than they do in Los Angeles. Comparative research can enable the manager or program implementer trying to transact business in a foreign culture to proceed circumspectly and effectively. To an ever increasing extent, however, organizational goals involve actively synchronizing operations within a variety of cultures. This is as true for the firm in Los Angeles trying to set up incentives for its multilingual work force as for the transnational firm trying to coordinate its production flow in six different countries. Such transactions involve recognition of and negotiation with multiple cultural systems.

The pitfalls for organizations attempting to juggle cultural multiplicity are legion. Everyone has heard, for example, of the disastrous General Motors promotion of its Chevy Nova in Mexico, in which no one had pointed out that, in Spanish, *No va* means "It doesn't go." The problems involved go deeper than understanding a simple relationship between words and what they refer to, however. If culture involves shared meanings, then moving in different cultures requires understanding different systems of meaning and the assumptions, principles, and nuances that any particular cultural object may evoke in these systems.

In his aptly titled book *Cultures in Conflict*, Stanley Heginbotham (1975) set out a memorable case of how lack of cultural coordination can undermine the most rationally conceived program. His subject was the implementation of the agricultural Green Revolution, specifically a high-yield variety of rice, in India. The plan was simple: Trained village workers called Gram Sevaks, under central coordination from New Delhi, were to serve as on-site agricultural extension officers. Their job was to convince the local farmers to try the new rice, along with new fertilizers and other farming techniques promoted by Green Revolution advocates. The problems came from the fact that four cultures and hence four distinct ways of thinking were engaged in the plan's implementation. Many of the higher level agricultural extension officers (AEOs) had been trained at such places as the University of Iowa and were aglow with American theories of community development and local empowerment. A Gandhian culture of individual responsibility animated some of the local extension workers. The Indian bureaucracy, however, still followed the British colonial model of tight central control and elaborated paper-passing, without much concern for the end results as long as the proper routines were carried out. The peasant farmers, meanwhile, operated under yet a fourth cultural model, that of traditional dharma, which emphasized doing one's duty and submitting to one's fate. Thus, the people responsible for implementing the program held four cognitive models—community development, Gandhian, colonial bureaucratic, and dharmaic. The first two models emphasized change and flexibility in order to meet specific goals; the second two stressed stability and following the correct procedure regardless of the consequences.

The results were predictably disastrous. Extension agents gave enthusiastic speeches about crop rotation to patient farmers who smiled and paid no attention, assuming the agents were simply performing some obscure duty. Bureaucrats sought to meet quotas on seed distribution without expressing any great interest in whether the seeds were actually planted. And the Gram Sevaks and extension officers improvised like crazy. In the case of "green manure"—a fast-growing, high foliage crop that farmers were to plant when the fields would otherwise be fallow, and then plow under to enrich the soil—most farmers were unpersuaded by the scientific rationale of soil improvement. To them, "green manure" sounded like a waste of time and energy. The extension officers had quotas of green manure seed distribution to fill, however, quotas established by the bureaucrats in New Delhi. So the AEOs and the Gram Sevaks induced the farmers to take the green manure seeds, which they did not want, in return for being able to buy cheap fertilizer, which they did. "As a result of such a quid pro quo," Heginbotham reported, "a farmer might count himself fortunate to have obtained a permit to buy fertilizer at a subsidized rate and an AEO would be relieved to have made progress toward fulfilling his target for the sale of green manure seeds nobody wanted. Neither would be particularly disturbed by the fact that the farmer would simply throw out the seeds" (p. 169).

Given the pitfalls of cultures in conflict, and given the increasing necessity for individuals and organizations to work in and with a variety of cultures, what help can cultural sociology offer? At the most basic level, it can focus attention on the fact that even a tangible, physical "thing" like fertilizer is a cultural object. As such, it is a bearer of meaning, but its meanings vary with the human beings—producers and recipients—who interact with it. Although everyone agrees that green manure is a seed for a type of plant, they most definitely do not agree about what it represents as a cultural object. Green manure was produced by Western scientists, to whom it meant one shot fired in a revolution in Third World agriculture. But it also meant low-cost organic fertilizers to the Gram Sevaks, more work to the farmer, and a means of furthering his civil service career to the bureaucrat. Once more we are reminded that meanings are not implanted in a cultural object; they are constructed by those human beings who interact with the object. An astute, culturally aware member of the implementation team might have anticipated some of these different meaning constructions and made provision for them.

The need to be alert to multiple meanings and culturally based nuances carries over to intangible cultural objects such as words. Considerable intercultural confusion comes from translations that, though accurate on a word-to-word basis, do not capture the nimbus of implications with which a culture surrounds a word. For example, President Clinton complained that the Japanese say yes when they mean no. A writer familiar with both cultures pointed out that *hai*, the Japanese equivalent of yes, can mean that the speaker has heard you and is weighing a reply or that the speaker understands your request and would like to accommodate you but unfortunately cannot (Hatsumi, 1993). A Japanese speaker is not intending to be deceitful in such "yes" responses, merely polite. Nigerians behave similarly when they have bad news to report. Because breaking bad news too abruptly is considered to be insensitive, if a Nigerian has news that the other party wants—the answer to a question such as "Is he dead?" or "Did the deal go through?"—he will often equivocate for some time, saying, "Things are well" or "The story is a complicated one," before telling the painful truth. Outsiders who understand such cultural patterns can avoid either misinterpreting the response or drawing the mistaken conclusion that the party with whom they are interacting is a liar.

The multiple interpretations of intangible cultural objects can be understood through the cultural diamond framework. A Japanese produces a *hai* as a cultural object; his period eye, his collective consciousness, imbue his *hai* with a set of meanings and implications. A Japanese recipient, coming from the same social world, would have no trouble comprehending his meaning. But an American, coming from a social world that overlaps but is not identical with that of the Japanese, has a different horizon of expectations. She constructs different meanings out of the cultural object *hai*, especially if it has been translated as a simple yes. A general rule might be this: In any situation wherein the creator of a cultural object and its receiver come from different cultures, an individual or organization must be alert at all times to the possibility of different meaning constructions, for these nonequivalent meanings may have significant consequences for "getting things done."

Summary

The international flows of people, goods, images, and information mean that virtually every organization must contend with cultural multiplicity. From the viewpoint of a business firm, a government agency, or other organization trying to get something done, multiple cultures are always potentially cultures in conflict. A sociological understanding of cultures and how they operate will help predict areas of conflict, reduce the conflict if possible, and manage it when it does arise.

In this chapter, we have considered the impact of culture on organizations at a number of levels:

1. Culture and motivation. Organizations need to motivate their employees to behave in ways beneficial to the organization's goals. Both internal subcultures of work groups and external cultural influences can interfere with this process by motivating different types of behavior. Management needs to create an organizational culture using some combination of structural means, recruitment, socialization, rituals, model actors, and illuminating stories so that the desired behavior becomes meaningful and satisfying to the employees.

2. Organizational subcultures. In spite of managerial efforts to exert normative control by creating an organizational culture, subcultures will emerge that to some extent resist the dominant culture. Such subcultures and the stories they tell will often reproduce social cleavages of class, ethnicity, and gender. Within a particular organization, each subculture is both a meaning-making unit, such as Fantasia's nurses, and a medium through which meanings from the external culture find expression and enactment. If we consider a new product, program, or policy as a cultural object, we can anticipate some of the different meanings that object will have for different groups and their implications for attitudes and behavior.

3. Cross-cultural differences. People's ways of thinking and acting vary enormously from place to place, and much scholarly ink has been spilled trying to assess the impact these variations have on organizational effectiveness. In the past, a culturalist model, which claimed that national or local cultural values explained organizational differences, opposed a structuralist model, which contended that similar organizational structures produced similar consequences regardless of culture. Recent thinking has moved beyond the either/or terms of these two models to explain how culture influences structure and how structures are interpreted through cultures.

4. Organizations in multicultural environments. Organizations that operate in more than one country or involve several cultural groups in a single country face multiple systems of meaning creation. Although managers cannot control the cognitive frames that will make their organization's products and programs meaningful in different cultures, they can first recognize this lack of control, rather than assume that the characteristics and meanings of something like a "Big Mac"

are transparent and unitary. Second, managers can anticipate when meaning construction will seriously challenge the goals of the organization and act in light of this understanding.

RECOMMENDED FOR FURTHER READING

Fantasia, Rick. 1988. *Cultures of Solidarity: Consciousness, Action, and Contemporary American Workers.* Berkeley: University of California Press. Rich case studies of the creation and reception of the image of worker solidarity as a cultural object.

Heginbotham, Stanley J. 1975. *Cultures in Conflict: The Four Faces of Indian Bureaucracy.* New York: Columbia University Press. An unusual comparative account of how four distinct cultures come to bear on a single program.

Hochschild, Arlie Russell. 1983. *The Managed Heart: Commercialization of Human Feeling.* Berkeley: University of California Press. How organizations control what Geertz calls the moods and motivations of its employees. Hochschild studied airlines, which train flight attendants to be nice, and collection agencies, which use similar techniques to train its employees to be mean.

Kunda, Gideon. 1992. *Engineering Culture: Control and Commitment in a High Tech Organization.* Philadelphia: Temple University Press. From ethnographic fieldwork, Kunda depicts an organization that is highly aware of its organizational culture and highly skilled at manipulating it.

Orrù, Marco; Biggart, Nicole Woolsey; and Hamilton, Gary G. 1991. "Organizational Isomorphism in East Asia." In *The New Institutionalism in Organizational Analysis.* Walter W. Powell and Paul J. DiMaggio, eds. Pp. 361-389. A comparative study showing how cultural assumptions have an impact on organizational forms and relationships.

7

Technology, Community, and Global Culture

Business transactions and interconnected social problems are just two of the many domains in which people have been linked together at an accelerating rate—economically, politically, socially, and culturally—throughout the twentieth century and into the twenty-first. Today, only a few isolated groups, deep in the disappearing rain forests or concealed in increasingly accessible mountain strongholds, are unaware of their connections with the rest of humanity. And even they are profoundly affected by these unseen connections. Pollution reaches them; national governments claim them; diseases jump geographic barriers to infect them; concerned citizens of the developed world, connected with one another through electronic mail, global conferences, and mailing lists, debate issues relating to their preservation and survival. Geographically remote people become cultural objects to hosts of unknown others.

If the world is becoming increasingly interconnected, does this mean we are moving toward a single homogeneous culture, what Marshall McLuhan once called a "global village"? Or does greater connectedness magnify the differences among societies? Like a cable television system that is accessible to every household but has a different channel for every conceivable taste, does the universal reach of the electronic media also generate a proliferation of fine distinctions and particularized local cultures? Paradoxically, both seem to be happening. Globalization is exerting simultaneous pressures toward unity and fragmentation.

In this chapter, we explore the paradox and consider its implications for culture and cultural meanings. We look at the relationship between culture, technology, and community in an effort to identify how changes in communication technologies have changed the nature of culture and how different cultural technologies have affected human communities and the very idea of community. We move from oral storytelling around the fire to literacy and then to the present era of electronic communications. Finally, returning to culture as the bearer of meanings, we consider the future of meaning in a global culture.

Cultural Technologies and Cultural Communities

Like culture, the word community has a number of meanings for sociologists, but two are paramount: community as a territorial concept, and community as a relational concept. In the first sense, a community is something we can locate on a map. It has spatial properties: borders, a center, outskirts. It also has a name and a set of symbols associated with it. Residents of Chicago know where the South Side and Lincoln Park are; they know the borders, the landmarks, the types of people who live in these communities. Communities are meaningful; they are cultural objects to their residents and to many nonresidents as well.

Community in its second sense is relational: Communities are people who are tied together by webs of communication, friendship, association, or mutual support. They may be scattered geographically, they may not even know one another, but they constitute a meaningful, self-aware collectivity. Thus, it makes sense to speak of the Jewish community, the gay community, the academic community. In the past, of course, there was considerable overlap between these two types of community. People who lived in the same town or village were also linked with one another through friendship, kinship, trade, shared beliefs, a common set of symbols. But in an increasingly mobile and highly differentiated society, there is less and less identity between relational and territorial communities.

A community may be bound by geography, or it may be bound by network links, but members of either type of community are united, at least to some extent, by culture. This does not imply that all community members share in an undifferentiated collective consciousness, but simply that some considerable numbers of shared meanings are recognized by the members of any collectivity we would call a community. A group of people waiting for a light to change do not constitute a community; they share some signs (they all know that red means stop), but not necessarily much else. Members of the gay community, the Jewish community, or the South Side community, on the other hand, share experiences, meanings, ways of thinking and acting, beliefs, cultural objects. Culture can bind a community for centuries even when social forces have scattered or suppressed its members; the history of the Jews or the Gypsies or the ethnic minorities under the Soviet Union gives strong evidence of this.

If we accept this Durkheimian argument that culture is the tie that binds, then we must ask: What happens to community in times of cultural revolution? This question is particularly pressing today, for we are in the midst of a major cultural revolution, that of the explosive growth in global electronic communications. The very nature of human thinking is being affected by this growth. Surprisingly enough, it isn't the first time. In fact, electronic communications represent the third major media revolution that has transformed culture and society. The first two were the phonetic alphabet and print, and like the revolution now underway, each of these earlier revolutions profoundly affected human communities.

Let us trace briefly the evolution of communications media and their impact on community. To do this, we must start at the beginning, before the technologies of literacy appeared, when culture was transmitted largely by people talking with one another.

Oral Cultures

For most of its history, humankind has lived in a strictly oral culture. Oral cultures, in which communication depends on face-to-face interaction, are characterized by widely shared knowledge throughout the community. Such cultures demand prodigious feats of memorization from a few memory specialists, who serve as repositories of group history and genealogy, but most knowledge is held in common and constantly reiterated. From this comes two more characteristics of oral cultures: first, the widespread use of proverbs (a residual is still found in African literature); second, the flourishing of epic poetry, for shared wisdom can be encoded in poetic rhythms and figures of speech as an aid to memory.

In oral cultures, vocabularies tended toward the concrete. They were elaborate where, and only where, they needed to be; because there were no dictionaries to "store" words, infrequently used words would simply drop out of the discourse. Similarly, history—as stored in human memory—would be modified to serve present needs. Early in the twentieth century, British colonialists wrote down that the Gonja of northern Ghana had seven chiefdoms; the Gonja said this was a legacy of Ndewura Jakpa, the founder of their state, who had seven sons. Sixty years later, when two of the political divisions had disappeared, the Gonja reported that Jakpa had five sons. In oral societies, "myth and history merge into one" (Goody & Watt, 1963, p. 311).

What type of community does oral culture support? Durkheim described it well: a small-scale, undifferentiated social order in which people think, do, and believe much the same things. In such communities, the overlap between an individual's consciousness and the collective consciousness is nearly total. Having little basis for comparing their own group's thinking with any other's, members of such a community would find their own way of life both stable and profoundly normal (as suggested by the common practice premodern groups had of simply calling themselves "the people").

Oral cultural communities are filled with magic, enchanted with mysterious forces and spirits. Because facts and histories lack fixity, the boundaries between reality and unreality are fluid, easily crossed. It is not surprising, for example, that magical realism has been a popular literary form in cultures such as Latin America and, increasingly, Africa, where the narrative patterns of oral culture are still strong.

Despite the profound changes literacy would bring to human communities, it did not simply sweep away oral culture. To a considerable extent, we still live in an oral world. The cultures of families, friendships, and neighborhoods are primarily oral, which may be why we place such value on letters, photographs, and other documentary traces of these cultures. Because these cultures are in what Cooley (1956) called "primary groups" in which the self is shaped, we can see the continuing power of orality. Moreover, much of the culture of institutions and organizations is oral, as in the stories told in the firms Joanne Martin (1992) studied. Nevertheless, literacy produced revolutionary upheavals in human culture and in the communities from which people took their identities. Let's turn now to this first revolution in communications technology.

The Impact of Literacy

Although phonetic writing systems developed in the New East some 3,000 years ago (Goody & Watt, 1963), other and earlier forms of writing had had their own social consequences. A number of nonphonetic writing systems—the Sumerian, the Egyptian, the Chinese—had already emerged in the ancient world in which signs stood for particular words, more or less on a one-to-one basis. Such systems are extremely complex, for literate people in these cultures must know thousands of signs in order to have a reading capacity that matches their spoken vocabulary. Classical Chinese, for example, has some 50,000 characters and takes about twenty years to learn. The result was that only a very small group of specialists, the religious or governmental elite, were literate in that society. Chinese society as a whole remained an oral culture, and the fundamental social distinction was between the literati, who administered the imperial bureaucracy, and everyone else.

Phonetic alphabets, in which characters represent sounds rather than words or concepts, are far simpler, and thus far easier to learn. In Western Europe and the United States, most three-year-olds can rattle off the 26 letters of our Roman alphabet. Such ease in learning encourages the general adoption of writing, especially among commercial classes. Popular literacy may be something of a misnomer—it was first established among the Greeks, but women and slaves were much less likely to be literate than free men—but nevertheless alphabetic scripts made possible a widespread participation in written culture. Literacy on this scale is generally taken as distinguishing modern from premodern societies; it has also traditionally distinguished the subject matter of sociology from that of anthropology.

The second, related communications revolution occurred in the fifteenth century, when a German printer named Johann Gutenberg invented movable type, which made possible written communication on a totally different scale from that which handwritten manuscripts could support. The shift from manuscript to print culture democratized literacy in the West and allowed for transmission and comparison of knowledge. In Europe, printing laid the technical basis for the Renaissance (print made classical texts widely available), the Reformation (now people could have and read their own Bibles, rather than having to depend on the interpretations of priests), and the rise of rationalized science (Eisenstein, 1979).[1] Because literacy became much more universal as a consequence of printing, we can say that print itself made modernity possible.

Goody and Watt (1963) suggested that two of the intellectual consequences of literacy are (1) the separation of history from myth—once a story has been written down, for example about Jakpa's seven sons, it becomes harder to change—and (2) an increased individualism based on highly specialized knowledge. In literate cultures, people are stratified on the basis of what they have read; academic disciplines and college majors are an obvious example of this kind of specialization. These are cognitive changes based on popular literacy, and they affect everyone in a literate society regardless of whether or not all members can actually read and write.

What about the impact of print, and the widespread literacy that it made possible, on community? First, literacy made relational communities possible as they had not been before. Because members of relational communities are not in regular face-to-face contact, they need some medium through which they can develop and preserve their sense of connection. The written word was that medium. Clearly, relational communities existed

---

[1]Printing was not a European invention; the Chinese had been making prints centuries before Gutenberg. But the lack of a phonetic alphabet severely limited the usefulness of printing in China (imagine setting type for 50,000 different characters), and print in the East had nothing like the impact it had in the West.

before printing—commercial traders exchanging goods and correspondence along a particular trading route, for example, and political or religious leaders communicating through manuscripts, letters (the apostle Paul didn't have a printing press but managed to put together a far-flung relational community with impressive staying power), and oral messengers—but printing and the proliferation of written materials made it possible for ordinary people to be members of any number of relational communities.

Second, printing brought forth an entirely new kind of territorial community, that of the nation. Benedict Anderson (1983) showed how national consciousness emerged in Western Europe from the seventeenth-century spread of vernacular languages in printed form, supplanting the former use of Latin as a common language for business and legal, as well as religious, matters. Now it became possible for people to conceive of other people, unseen and unknown, who read the same materials, knew the same things, shared the same cultural objects. A language community would not have to be territorially connected, of course, but most vernacular languages were; hence, the nation took on a territorial, as well as a linguistic, specificity. New print genres, especially the newspaper and the novel, were both cause and consequence of the spread of nationalism as an idea and of particular national identities.

So the print revolution gave rise to relational communities connected by the written, and especially the published, word, and it gave rise to that very modern form of territorial human organization, the nation-state. Of course, print helped establish and bind together smaller communities as well, for example with local newspapers for territorial communities and mailed newsletters for relational communities. All of this is familiar to us, for print culture has shaped the world in which we live. But what will happen to this familiar world when print is superseded?

Electronic Media

Electronic communications, including broadcasting, mark the third great revolution in human communications and move us from the modern into the postmodern era. This revolution includes two-way transmission (telegraph, telephone, fax, computer networks, electronic mail), as well as one-way transmission (radio, television, audio- and videocassettes). All of these technologies have a number of common attributes:

1. They connect people in separate locations with no lapse in time.

2. They allow the raw expression of ideas and emotions, making possible an immediacy and intimacy that had previously occurred only in face-to-face communication.
3. They democratize cultural access in spatial and temporal terms. A cultural event such as a concert is no longer fixed to one time and one location; when it is recorded on tape, the receiver can select when and where to listen.
4. They democratize cultural access based on education. Whereas written communications require mastery of a set of skills, many forms of electronic communication—especially television and telephone—require far fewer skills. Virtually any competent human can master and use them. A two-year-old can attend to and "follow" a television program; a functional illiterate who previously would have been totally excluded from the world of newspapers can receive news on the radio; an unschooled man can make his views known over the telephone or on a talk show.

The social consequences of electronic media flow from these attributes, often in rather unexpected ways. Because of the breadth of the electronic audience and the speed with which messages may be sent to them, influencing public opinion through the media has become a key objective of those promoting a certain political or social program. Exiled political leaders use media to encourage and rally their supporters, as Ayatollah Khomeini did with tapes of his addresses. Government officials use the media to sell and justify their actions: When the 1993 standoff between the Branch Davidian cult and the FBI in Waco ended in disaster, Attorney General Janet Reno spent days on interview and talk shows explaining the government's actions and reasoning. The series of political revolutions in Eastern Europe in which country after country threw off Communist governments were linked by television and fax machines; Lech Walesa, when asked what had caused the collapse of communism, pointed to a television set (Lippman, 1992). Civil rights movement leaders in the late 1950s and 1960s recognized and made effective use of television's capacity to awaken revulsion in viewers, who were moved by images of police dogs attacking unarmed marchers in a way they had not been by years of printed newspaper reports of lynchings and other racial atrocities. Todd Gitlin (1980) used an apt phrase from the anti-Vietnam war movement to describe that movement's use of television, one that applies generally to any social movement that can attract the media: "The whole world is watching."

Electronic media increase not only the immediacy of human contacts, but also their intimacy. This effect was unanticipated. Claude Fischer (1992), for example, studied the history of the telephone in America. Originally, the Bell System assumed that its product would be used primarily by commercial firms to conduct their business transactions. To everyone's surprise, the fastest growth of telephone subscribers came from private homes, especially those of rural women eager to be in touch with relatives and friends. In this sense, the telephone contributed to the preservation of relational communities; computer networks, faxes, and E-mail continue to do the same today.

The possibility of immediate and intimate communications has broken down a number of long-standing social barriers (Meyrowitz, 1985). Now it is common for lifestyles that were formerly hidden from mainstream view, the subject of rumor but little knowledge, to parade openly and loquaciously on the radio and television talk shows. Now raw, unedited human responses—the politician snarling at reporters after his bill has been defeated, the parents sobbing when their child has been killed in a gang shoot-out—are shared with millions of total strangers. Such direct contact with the personal lives of strangers has contributed to an increasing informality of human relations. Whether or not it has led to greater tolerance, as Matthew Arnold dreamed, is another question, however. Human differences and human emotions have become entertainment. As the mass culture theorists predicted, the continued presence of suffering may have dulled our sensitivity to it.

The visual representation of starvation offers an example. Probably the first effective use of what might be called the public relations of hunger was mounted by Biafran government officials during the Nigerian civil war of the late 1960s. Pictures of children with the bloated stomachs caused by kwashiorkor, a disease caused by a deficiency in protein, arouse concern and some considerable support for Biafra in Europe and the United States. But in the 1970s and 1980s, when Africa experienced a series of droughts and war-created famines, images of starving children became familiar, even conventional. In 1992, it took months of such pictures and reports to stimulate world response to the starvation produced by fighting between warlords in Somalia.

The third and fourth attributes, the democratizing impact of media, also have had profound social effects. Print tends to segment audiences: Different groups of people read different books. Similarly, the traditional concentration of intellectuals, universities, theaters, cathedrals, and other cultural institutions in a few cities formerly meant that there were cultural centers and peripheries. This is now changing. Television, because of the minimal skills or effort required to decode its meanings and because of its virtually universal access, tends to be watched by huge, widespread, and undifferentiated audiences. In theory, cable programming, with its almost unlimited choice possibilities, could segment audiences into discrete taste cultures, but this effect does not seem to have happened. Research shows that infrequent television viewers, when they do turn on the set, watch the most popular shows; heavy viewers watch the popular shows and some of the highly specialized ones as well.

Let's consider one example of the impact that electronic communications are having. Half a century after its Communist revolution, China faces a new revolution, that of communication media. Chinese leaders have traditionally emphasized the relationship between knowledge and political power more than most countries and have taken great pains to control it. The Chinese Communist Party has striven to monopolize news and propaganda, particularly in the delicate post-Tiananmen Square era as they attempt to foster economic change (capitalism) without political change (democracy). But their monopoly is crumbling, and the culprit is technology (Kristof, 1993). Satellite dishes are sprouting "like bamboo shoots after a spring rain," enabling viewers to tune in everything from BBC news to Michael Jackson on MTV.

The government attempts to control the proliferation of the dishes; theoretically, one needs police permission to watch anything but China's own programs. Top government position papers rail against foreign programs for being pornographic and/or politically reactionary. But control of the airwaves is virtually impossible, and the Chinese remain unimpressed by their government's efforts. " 'When I bought my dish, the salesman told me that if the police ever asked, I should tell them that I use it only to watch China Central Television,' said a 28-year-old businessman who bought his dish a few months ago. 'The police know that's absurd, but they can't prove it' " (Kristof, 1993).

Thanks to new technologies, the flow of new images and ideas cannot be stopped, even in a police state. And although most Chinese viewers are primarily attracted to mass cultural products such as sitcoms and soap operas, even these can be enlightening in a country where political suppression has been the rule. "American cops-and-robbers shows sometimes play on Chinese television, and viewers often find the plot twists full of surprises—like the moments when the bad guys are read their rights and allowed to call a lawyer. To some Chinese, that kind of novelty is more memorable than the plot itself" (Kristof, 1993).

Examples such as this highlight the impact that electronic communications are having. Clearly, one of the consequences will be that nation-states such as China will find it increasingly difficult to intercept foreign cultural messages at their boundaries. If communities are bound by cultures, and if national cultures are increasingly penetrated from outside, then "global culture" displaces "national culture" to an ever greater extent. Does this mean the world will soon all be one happy community? Few theorists, either of contemporary society or of postmodernity, have been optimistic, as we see in the following section.

Communities of Meaning in a Global Culture

Robert Bellah and his colleagues (1984) used the expression "lifestyle enclaves" to describe the places where people can choose to live with others just like them. They point out that, formerly, people lived and interacted with different types of people (in age, occupation, family form) in their communities. Now, if people select to live in communities where only retired people who like golf live, or only young, childless professionals live, they can do so. Bellah sees this development as a failure of the Durkheimian organic exchange that should take place in modern communities.

Similarly, people can now live within what we might call "cultural enclaves." Individuals with very different meaning systems—from cyberpunks to fundamentalist Muslims—can create and receive their own distinct cultural objects and confine their interactions to those others who share their meaning systems. These interacting cultural groups may be labeled communities, and they may and do cross political and geographical boundaries, but they are built around sameness rather than around diversity. Their tendency is not to increase tolerance—the stated goal of multiculturalism—but to diminish it.

Bellah's lifestyle enclaves were geographical, but the process of separation is even more pronounced for relational communities. Mexican soccer fans can watch Spanish-language soccer games 24 hours a day. They can contact other soccer aficionados on computer networks to share information and debate fine points of the game. Through developments in virtual reality, they soon may be able to amuse themselves by simulations that allow them to experience actually playing the game. Such individuals could maintain this cultural enclave, a tight relational community (or self-designed ghetto) anywhere in the world they happened to live. Once again, the paradox: Just as electronic globalization seems to unite people geographically, it also seems to separate them relationally. On the one hand, a global village; on the other, the self-absorbed worlds of the soccer fans and other cultural enclaves. Both are communities, but both seem to lack depth. And this—say theorists of postmodernity much taken with these developments—is the whole point.

Postmodernity and Community

Global electronic communications, with their infinite capacity for the reproduction and dissemination of signs, are the foundation of postmodernism. Postmodern culture is a culture of surfaces, a play of images denying depth, history, or meaning. It has been characterized as having the following attributes (Harvey, 1989; Jameson, 1984):

- Depthlessness, a self-aware superficiality. Depth has been replaced by multiple surfaces. There are no hidden meanings, for indeed there is nothing beneath the glittering surfaces that the culture presents. The mirrored sunglasses or the mirrored surface of a building are exemplary postmodern cultural objects, denying depth or meaning within, stopping visual penetration at the surface, throwing back the image of the beholder.

- The rejection of metanarratives, which we discuss in Chapter 5. One aspect of this is a weakened sense of national history or destiny. To speak of a concept such as American destiny or the inevitable triumph of socialism today would be to sound embarrassingly naive. Frederick Jameson (1984) described it:

    The advanced capitalist countries today are now a field of stylistic and discursive heterogeneity without a norm. Faceless masters continue to inflect the economic strategies which constrain our existences, but they no longer need to impose their speech (or are henceforth unable to): and the postliteracy of the late capitalist world reflects not only the absence of any great collective project but also the unavailability of the older national language itself. (p. 17)

- Fragmentation, the breakdown of connections. Postmodern culture embraces the fragmentary, the ephemeral, the discontinuous. Pastiche, the splicing together of cultural elements from different times and places, is a convention of postmodernist art and literature. This technique holds echoes of the cultural bricoleur discussed in Chapter 4, but the bricoleur is trying to accomplish something with the jerry-rigged construction. Postmodern pastiche has no such end in mind.

Now a culture that denies depth and history, a culture that rejects any larger story of its past and future, a culture wherein anything can be combined with anything else—such a culture, to put it mildly, does not sound promising as a foundation around which community can be built. What can we conclude about the relationship between electronic media and global postmodern culture on the one hand, and the possibility for community on the other? The question is not an idle one for sociology. A century ago, men who worried about the corrosive effects that modernity—rationalization, capitalism, anomie—would have on human community were the founders of the discipline. In their various social theories, they envisioned the type of ties that could bind people and give their lives meaning in the contemporary world. For Marx, it was class consciousness; for Weber, it was systems of ideas; for Durkheim, it was some embodiment of the collective conscience. All of these thinkers proposed cultural meaning-producing systems that might offer a defense against the individualistic, dog-eat-dog world of their society.

These founders of sociology looked ahead to the twentieth century; we now look to the twenty-first. Electronic media have made it possible to put human beings in touch with one another as never before. The global circulation of money and people has been accompanied, and even preceded, by a circulation of cultural objects trailing shreds of meanings behind them. Will this course have a unifying effect? Will cultural sharing at last achieve Matthew Arnold's dream of a tolerant and reasonable human community?

The cultural theories we have discussed give basis for both optimism and pessimism. On the optimistic side, community and a sense of solidarity come from interaction, for it is through interactions with others that we, like Fine's Little Leaguers, build up shared meaning systems. Charles Cooley (1956) wrote that primary groups, those groups such as the family and neighborhood where we have our earliest and most intimate interactions, form people's sense of who they are and with whom they are identified. Extending Cooley's reasoning, if electronic communications make intimate interactions possible for more and more people regardless of where they are physically located, it may lead to a greater communion among them, a greater sense of what they have in common as people. Recall that when Americans and Europeans watched the CNN reports of the Gulf War in 1991, they shared a heightened sense of all being "in this together." Could communications foster a global sense of "all being in this together?"

Perhaps. Sociology counters its own optimism with darker views, however. Durkheim pointed out the paradox that in a society with a highly advanced division of labor, the only thing people have in common is their individualism. Today, we have the technological means to give rich cultural expression to that individualism. In fact, recent years have produced an explosion of cultural forms serving highly specialized groups and interests: desktop publishing, computer networks, 'zines, cable television channels, the decline of "top 40" radio stations in favor of segmented stations for hip hop, soft rock, contemporary country, rap, salsa. Plugged into their Walkmans, selecting their own videos, interacting with their special computer networks, people can increasingly dwell in cultural ghettos of their own choosing.

Some sociologists have suggested that the need to erect and emphasize cultural boundaries is a response to pressure on other boundaries. The general idea is that external pressure on a society will bring about a greater emphasis on internal hierarchies, as well as on defending the distinctions perceived to be threatened. Christie Davies (1982) showed this to be true for deviant sexuality. There are always rules and laws against tabooed sexual behavior such as homosexuality, bestiality, or cross-dressing, but these laws are not always enforced. His historical analysis shows that it is precisely when groups come under pressure from outside that they become obsessed with purifying internal categories, such as the distinctions between male and female or human and animal, and one sign of this obsession is a stepped-up enforcement of sex codes.

A more general statement of Davies's point would be that when institutions and meaning systems are threatened or disrupted, it may not be the case that entirely new ones will be created; one response may simply be a greater emphasis on preexisting cultural traits and distinctions. Thus Wuthnow's (1987) "breakdowns in the moral order" may not produce new ideologies; it may reinvigorate old ones, including old hatreds that were assumed to have vanished from the modern world. The increasing fragmentation and resurgent ethnicity of the former Eastern bloc gives evidence of this. The concept of "ethnic cleansing" represents community with a vengeance.

But it may be that we have posed the issue incorrectly. Spatial and relational communities are nothing new, and the fact that electronic communications have multiplied the latter does not necessarily mean the eclipse of the former; community is not a zero-sum game, nor is meaning. Theorists of postmodernity may have missed something: We may, in fact, witness a proliferation of both surfaces and depths. Human beings may well learn to operate simultaneously in global, relational communities and in local, spatial ones. Each community will have its own culture. Let us conclude by considering what such a world would look like.

Speaking in Tongues

It is increasingly common for people to describe themselves as speaking parallel languages. Chicano writer Richard Rodriguez (1982) described, for example, how English was his language for public communication, Spanish his language of private intimacy. Perry Link (1992) wrote about how Chinese intellectuals self-consciously manage a dual discourse: the public language that repeats the party line, the private language that mocks the public. Nigerian novelists may address their readers in English, their literary correspondents in French, their children in Yoruba, their servants in pidgin; they report no difficulty, for each language seems suited to its context and task.

In all of these examples, we can see the public languages as speaking to a relational community, the private languages as addressing a spatial community. The former is specific, task oriented, formal, impersonal; the latter is diffuse, intimate. Instead of language, however, suppose we substitute culture. Now we have the image of a postmodern, electronically plugged-in individual who can share cultural objects, communicate signs and perhaps symbols as well, in a variety of relational communities, unhindered by space or time. This same individual shares cultural objects in one or more local communities, communities of face-to-face contact and some considerable intimacy There is no reason to suppose that this person would experience one form of cultural community as overwhelming or displacing any other in her life.

In fact, the opposite may be true. Electronic media and the global relational communities they establish may strengthen ties at the local level. When the Israeli television watchers discussed the program *Dallas* for Leibes and Katz, as discussed in Chapter 4, they were responding to a single cultural object, electronically produced and transmitted globally. In their responses, however, group members enacted their shared horizons of expectations, thus confirming to themselves and to one another what it meant to be, for example, a Russian Jew. In interacting with a single cultural object, they participated in both intensified global and intensified local culture. A modernist account of the cultural stresses and psychic disruptions of emigration would tell only part of their cultural story; so would a postmodern analysis of *Dallas* as signs without referents.

Let's stay in Israel, but go back 2,000 years. The New Testament book of Acts tells us that when the spirit came upon the disciples at Pentecost, they began speaking in tongues. Jews from all over the Mediterranean world who had gathered in Jerusalem for the Pentecost celebration heard them. These Jews, multicultural and speaking many languages, were amazed that they could all understand the disciples; even though the disciples were Galileans, each Jewish visitor seemed to hear them speaking in his or her own language. It is not clear what language the disciples were actually speaking (some scoffers at the scene maintained that they were just drunk), but the miracle lay in the fact that listeners who did not speak their language were able to understand them. Some cultural objects —maybe they were meaningful to their creators, maybe they were just drunken babble after all—were received by some people having specific horizons of expectations and accordingly became meaningful.

Drawing an analogy from the Bible to make a point about postmodern culture is, in itself, a very postmodern move. What we want to suggest is that electronic media make cultural objects widely available, accessible across the globe (no more traveling to Jerusalem necessary). People who are, after all, located in time and space can now interact with these cultural objects to make meanings. And these meanings must speak to them and their groups in their own languages. Thus, we have breadth and depth, a collective representation across a relational community and a collective representation of a local community, mass communication, and popular meaning-making. Shared meaning (shared locally) embodied in form (transmitted globally)—that's what cultural objects are all about.

Cultures Without Centers

At the dawn of the twentieth century, William Butler Yeats made a double prediction in one poetic line. I cited this before, but it bears repeating: "Things fall apart, the centre cannot hold." Now, at the dawn of a new century, we realize he was half right. Cultural centers did not hold. We have gone from a bipolar to a polycentric world, from a world of cultural hierarchies to a world of multiple and parallel meaning systems, from a world where specialists controlled access to information to a world where "the best that has been thought and known," and the worst too, is accessible to all.

At the same time, however, things did not fall apart. Human beings continue to ward off chaos through cultural objects; the embrace of chaos tends to be a temporary and highly stylized posture of youth, like the jackets embroidered with "Live fast, die young." People continue to produce and perpetuate their cultures through interaction and socialization. Our original cultural definitions still work. People may exist in multiple communities through multiple networks, but along these networks they still share meanings with one another. Communities, whether relational or spatial, still collectively represent themselves through patterns of meanings embodied in symbols, meanings that shape attitudes and actions.

In a decentered world, understanding the connections among cultures and societies may require a handful of cultural diamonds, but the familiar questions still apply. To understand any cultural phenomenon, from the traditional to the postmodern, one needs to ask: What are the characteristics of this specific cultural object? What does it mean, and for whom? Who are its creators? Who are its receivers, and how do they interpret it? From what social world does it come, and into what social world is it sent? One can ask these questions about an MTV video or an idea sent through the internet just as one can ask them about a Chinese poem or a Nigerian masquerade. Their answers will continue to be revealing about the relevant social world. And those people who can come up with the answers will be those best equipped to navigate in the new century.

RECOMMENDED FOR FURTHER READING

Anderson, Benedict. (1983) 1991. *Imagined Communities: Reflections on the Origin and Spread of Nationalism* rev. ed. London: Verso. Anderson offers a masterly historical account of the rise of the nation as a cultural object.

Bellah, Robert N.; Madsen, Richard; Sullivan, William M.; Swidler, Ann; and Tipton, Steven M. 1984. *Habits of the Heart: Individualism and Commitment in American Life.* Berkeley: University of California Press. A disturbing analysis of the corrosive individualism that lies at the core of American public life and private relationships.

Goody, Jack and Watt, Ian. 1963. "The Consequences of Literacy." *Comparative Studies in Society and History* 5: 304-345. This influential paper about the consequences of alphabetic writing systems generated a continuing line of research supporting and rebutting its thesis.

Harvey, David. 1989. *The Condition of Postmodernity: An Enquiry Into the Origins of Cultural Change.* Oxford: Basil Blackwell. Harvey offers one of the most complete depictions of the causes and characteristics of postmodernity, while remaining critical of its political nihilism.

Link, E. Perry. 1992. *Evening Chats in Beijing: Probing China's Predicament.* New York: Norton. Link interviewed a great many Chinese intellectuals in the year ending with the Tiananmen Square massacre. He presents an absorbing portrait of thoughtful, creative people struggling to be true to their convictions in a repressive society.

Meyrowitz, Joshua. 1985. *No Sense of Place: The Impact of Electronic Media on Social Behavior.* New York: Oxford University Press. An insightful attempt to consider the social consequences of the third communications revolution.

Nigeria and China, Moving Into the Twenty-First Century

As suggested in the preface, Nigeria and China at the end of the twentieth century offer thought-provoking comparisons with the more familiar cultural patterns and changes in the United States and Western Europe. In this appendix, I give a thumbnail sketch of the social composition and cultural heritage of these two important countries. For further reading, I recommend the rich portrait of modern China given by Spence (1990); for Nigeria, the reader should consult Crowder (1978) for a straightforward history and Achebe (1984) for a discussion of Nigeria's social and political tensions as viewed by one of its leading intellectuals.

Nigeria

With a population of some 90 million people, the Federal Republic of Nigeria is by far the most populous country in Africa. Located on the southern coast of West Africa, geographically Nigeria is more than twice the size of California. Its topography ranges from mangrove swamps in the south through rain forest, open grasslands, and finally semidesert in the north. Oil dominates its exports, and oil revenues have made possible its massive, but very uneven, development.

Advanced cultures have flourished in Nigeria for centuries, including the Yoruba and Benin kingdoms of the south and the Hausa states of the Islamic north. Britain seized control during the late nineteenth century and established the boundaries and the name of present-day Nigeria in 1914. The nation assumed its independence in 1960. After years of political turmoil, eastern Nigeria seceded in 1967, proclaiming itself the Republic of Biafra. This change triggered a civil war that may have cost as many as a million lives; the war ended in 1970 when Biafra surrendered and rejoined Nigeria. In its more than three decades of independence,

Nigeria has had a military government for all but nine years. Its leaders continue to work toward attaining a lasting democracy.

Nigeria has three major ethnic groups and hundreds of smaller ones. In the north, the Hausa dominate; in the southwest, the Yoruba; and in the southeast, the Igbo. The north is largely Islamic, while the south is predominantly Christian and animist. Ethnic and religious rivalries infiltrate the nation's political and social life and occasionally flare up into riots or massacres despite the efforts of the government and opinion leaders to defuse such tensions.

Its relatively high level of material resources and education, as well as its ethnic diversity, has produced in Nigeria a rich and varied culture. Nigerians have been especially prominent in literature—Wole Soyinka won the Nobel Prize in 1987, and Ben Okri won the Booker Prize for his novel *The Famished Road* in 1991—and in folk theater, especially in the Yoruba regions. Age-old arts of sculpture, weaving, and mask making are preserved, and states sponsor "cultural troupes" of traditional dancers and musicians. At the same time, Nigerians participate in the latest forms of popular culture, as in their Afro-pop singers, such as Sunny Ade, who command a worldwide following, and in their innovative television programs. Despite occasional attempts at censorship, the Nigerian press prides itself on being both free and critical.

China

China is the largest country in the world in population; with more than 1.1 billion people, the Chinese comprise 21% of the world's people. It is massive in geographic size as well, topped only by Russia and Canada. Although three-quarters of the Chinese live in rural areas, only one-tenth of the land is cultivated, with desert or mountains covering most of the rest. Its major industries include steel, textiles, and truck manufacture.

Chinese ruling dynasties can be traced back 3,000 years. The last dynasty, the Qing, lost control of the country during the nineteenth century, which saw foreign incursions, wars, and internal rebellions; the Qing ended in 1912 when China, under the leadership of Sun Yat-sen, became a republic. Bitter struggles between the nationalists and the communists, only temporarily suspended during the Japanese occupation during World War II, ended with the victory of the communist forces in 1949 under Mao Zedong. The communist rule has been punctuated by periods of ideological purification, such as the Cultural Revolution of the late 1960s, and periods of pragmatic economic development, such as the privatization reforms under Deng Xiaoping during the 1980s. Although still nominally a socialist economy, China's leaders are attempting to foster economic development along capitalist lines while restraining the attendant impulse toward democratization. This internally contradictory policy came to a head during the Tiananmen Square pro-democracy demonstration in 1989, when a huge crowd of students and workers demanding reforms was crushed by the army. The conflict between economic liberalization and political authoritarianism continues.

More than 90% of the Chinese are ethnically Han. Mandarin is the official language, although there are numerous regional dialects. China is officially atheist at present, but its religious traditions include Confucianism, Taoism, and Buddhism; recently there has been some revival of the Christianity introduced by nineteenth-century missionaries.

Chinese writers have been a major literary force for centuries; writers are both revered and feared by the Chinese regimes for their political influence. Other traditional arts include pottery, painting, and silk weaving. China has embraced electronic media; currently there is one television for every eight people. Changes in consumerism reveal this enthusiasm for electronics; under Mao, the "Four Musts" were a bicycle, a radio, a watch, and a sewing machine, and now the "Eight Bigs" desired by newly affluent Chinese are a color television, a stereo, a refrigerator, a camera, a motorcycle, a furniture suite, a washing machine, and an electric fan.

Some comparisons between China and Nigeria suggest their relative development. In China, the infant mortality rate is 33 per thousand live births, the life expectancy for women is 72 years, and the literacy rate is 70%. In Nigeria, the infant mortality rate is 118 per thousand, the female life expectancy is 50 years, and the literacy rate is (generously) estimated to be 50%. Neither China nor Nigeria is among the poorest nations of the world, but neither approaches the development of advanced industrial nations; Japan, for example, has an infant mortality rate of 4 per thousand, a female life expectancy of 82 years, and a 99% literacy rate.

References

Achebe, Chinua. 1958. *Things Fall Apart*. London: Heinemann.

Achebe, Chinua. 1984. *The Trouble With Nigeria*. London: Heinemann.

Anderson, Benedict. (1983) 1991. *Imagined Communities: Reflections on the Origin and Spread of Nationalism* rev. ed. London: Verso.

Anderson, Elijah. 1990. *Streetwise: Race, Class, and Change in an Urban Community*. Chicago: University of Chicago Press.

Appadurai, Arjun. 1990. "Disjuncture and Difference in the Global Cultural Economy." *Public Culture* 2: 1-24.

Arjomand, Said Amir. 1988. *The Turban for the Crown: The Islamic Revolution in Iran*. New York: Oxford University Press.

Arnold, Matthew. (1869) 1949. "Culture and Anarchy." In *The Portable Matthew Arnold*. Lionel Trilling, ed. New York: Viking.

Barnard, Chester A. 1939. *The Functions of the Executive*. Cambridge, MA: Harvard University Press.

Bastian, Misty L. 1992. "The Lure of the Roads." In *The World as Marketplace: Historical, Cosmological, and Popular Constructions of the Onitsha Market System*. University of Chicago: Unpublished doctoral dissertation. Pp. 99-254.

Baxandall, Michael. 1972. *Painting and Experience in Fifteenth-Century Italy*. New York: Oxford University Press.

Becker, Howard S. 1953. "Becoming a Marihuana User." *American Journal of Sociology* 59: 235-242.

Becker, Howard S. 1982. *Art Worlds*. Berkeley: University of California Press.

Beisel, Nicola. 1990. "Class, Culture, and Campaigns Against Vice in Three American Cities, 1872-1892." *American Sociological Review* 55: 44-62.

Bellah, Robert N.; Madsen, Richard; Sullivan, William M.; Swidler, Ann; and Tipton, Steven M. 1984. *Habits of the Hearth: Individualism and Commitment in American Life*. Berkeley: University of California Press.

Benson, Susan Porter. 1986. *Counter Cultures: Saleswomen, Managers, and Customers in American Department Stores, 1890-1940*. Urbana: University of Illinois Press.

Berger, Peter L. 1969. *The Sacred Canopy: Elements of a Sociological Theory of Religion*. New York: Author.

Bernstein, Basil. 1971. *Class, Codes, and Control*. London: Routledge & Kegan Paul.

Bourdieu, Pierre. 1984. *Distinction: A Social Critique of the Judgment of Taste.* Richard Nice, trans. Cambridge, MA: Harvard University Press.

Burns, Tom and Stalker, G. M. 1961. *The Management of Innovation.* London: Tavistock.

Cooley, Charles Horton. (1902) 1964. *Human Nature and the Social Order.* New York: Schocken.

Cooley, Charles Horton. 1956. *Social Organization.* Glencoe, IL: Free Press.

Cornell, Stephen. 1988. *The Return of the Native: American Indian Political Resurgence.* New York: Oxford University Press.

Crowder, Michael. 1978. *The Story of Nigeria* 4th ed. London: Faber & Faber.

Crozier, Michel. 1964. *The Bureaucratic Phenomenon.* Chicago: University of Chicago Press.

Davies, Christie. 1982. "Sexual Taboos and Social Boundaries." *American Journal of Sociology* 87: 1031-1063.

DiMaggio, Paul. 1987. "Classification in Art." *American Sociological Review* 52: 440-455.

DiMaggio, Paul and Mohr, John. 1985. "Cultural Capital, Educational Attainment, and Marital Selection." *American Journal of Sociology* 90: 1231-1261.

Dore, Ronald Philip. 1973. *British Factory, Japanese Factory: The Origins of National Diversity in Industrial Relations.* Berkeley: University of California Press.

Dorning, Mike. 1993. "Upset Stirs Fight for Irish Readers." *Chicago Tribune* May 3.

Durkheim, Emile. (1915) 1965. *The Elementary Forms of the Religious Life.* Joseph Ward Swain, trans. New York: Free Press.

Eisenstein, Elizabeth A. 1979. *The Printing Press as an Agent of Change: Communications and Cultural Transformations in Early-Modern Europe.* Cambridge, UK: Cambridge University Press.

Esherick, Joseph W. 1987. *The Origins of the Boxer Uprising.* Berkeley: University of California Press.

Fabricant, Florence. 1992. "Fresh From the Baker, a New Staff of Life." *New York Times* November 11.

Fantasia, Rick. 1988. *Cultures of Solidarity: Consciousness, Action, and Contemporary American Workers.* Berkeley: University of California Press.

Faulkner, Robert R. and Anderson, Andy B. 1987. "Short-Term Projects and Emergent Careers: Evidence From Hollywood." *American Journal of Sociology* 92: 879-909.

Fine, Gary Alan. 1987. *With the Boys: Little League Baseball and Preadolescent Culture.* Chicago: University of Chicago Press.

Fischer, Claude S. 1992. *America Calling: A Social History of the Telephone to 1940.* Berkeley: University of California Press.

Fischer, J. L. (1961) 1970. "Art Styles as Cultural Cognitive Maps." In *The Sociology of Art and Literature.* Milston C. Albrecht, James H. Barnett, and Mason Griff, eds. New York: Praeger. Pp. 72-89.

Fiske, John. 1989. *Understanding Popular Culture.* Boston: Unwin Hyman.

Gans, Herbert J. 1974. *Popular Culture and High Culture: An Analysis and Evaluation of Taste.* New York: Basic Books.

Geertz, Clifford. 1973. "Religion as a Cultural System." In *The Interpretation of Cultures.* New York: Basic Books.

Ginsberg, Faye. 1989. *Contested Lives: The Abortion Debate in an American Community.* Berkeley: University of California Press.

Gitlin, Todd. 1980. *The Whole World Is Watching: Mass Media in the Making and Unmaking of the New Left.* Berkeley: University of California Press.

Goffman, Erving. 1959. *The Presentation of Self in Everyday Life.* Garden City, NY: Doubleday.

Goldstone, Jack A. 1991. *Revolution and Rebellion in the Early Modern World.* Berkeley: University of California Press.

Goody, Jack and Watt, Ian. 1963. "The Consequences of Literacy." *Comparative Studies in Society and History* 5: 304-345.

Grauerholz, Elizabeth and Pescosolido, Bernice A. 1989. "Gender Representation in Children's Literature: 1900-1984." *Gender & Society* 3: 113-125.

Grayburn, Nelson H. 1967. "The Eskimos and 'Airport Art.' " *Trans action* (October): 28-33.

Greenfeld, Liah. 1989. *Different Worlds: A Sociological Study of Taste, Choice, and Success in Art.* Cambridge, UK: Cambridge University Press.

Griswold, Wendy. 1981. "American Character and the American Novel." *American Journal of Sociology* 86: 740-765.

Griswold, Wendy. 1986. *Renaissance Revivals: City Comedy and Revenge Tragedy in the London Theatre 1576-1980.* Chicago: University of Chicago Press.

Griswold, Wendy. 1987. "The Fabrication of Meaning: Literary Interpretation in the United States, Great Britain, and the West Indies." *American Journal of Sociology* 92: 1077-1117.

Gusfield, Joseph R. 1981. *The Culture of Public Problems: Drinking-Driving and the Symbolic Order.* Chicago: University of Chicago Press.

Haberman, Clyde. 1993. "Dishing Up Lunch for a Land That Isn't All Kosher." *New York Times* April 16.

Harrison, J. Richard and Carrroll, Glenn R. 1991. "Keeping the Faith: A Model of Cultural Transmission in Formal Organizations." *Administrative Science Quarterly* 36: 552-582.

Harvey, David. 1989. *The Condition of Postmodernity: An Enquiry Into the Origins of Cultural Change.* Oxford: Basil Blackwell.

Hatsumi, Reiko. 1993. "A Simple 'Hai' Won't Do." *New York Times* April 15.

Heginbotham, Stanley J. 1975. *Cultures in Conflict: The Four Faces of Indian Bureaucracy.* New York: Columbia University Press.

Hilgartner, Stephen and Bosk, Charles L. 1988. "The Rise and Fall of Social Problems: A Public Arenas Model." *American Journal of Sociology* 94: 53-78.

Hirsch, Paul M. 1972. "Processing Fads and Fashions: An Organization Set Analysis of Culture Industry Systems." *American Journal of Sociology* 77: 639-659.

Hochschild, Arlie Russell. 1983. *The Managed Heart: Commercialization of Human Feeling.* Berkeley: University of California Press.

Holland, Dorothy C. and Eisenhart, Margaret A. 1990. *Educated in Romance: Women, Achievement, and College Culture.* Chicago: University of Chicago Press.

Homans, George C. 1950. *The Human Group.* New York: Harcourt, Brace & World.

Hundley, Tom. 1993. "Mosque's Destruction Unleashes Host of India's Factional, Religious Horrors." *Chicago Tribune* January 17.

Hunter, James Davison. 1991. *Culture Wars: The Struggle to Define America.* New York: Basic Books.

Jackall, Robert. 1988. *Moral Mazes: The World of Corporate Managers.* New York: Oxford University Press.

Jaeger, Gertrude and Selznick, Philip. 1964. "A Normative Theory of Culture." *American Sociological Review* 29: 653-669.

Jameson, Frederick. 1984. "Postmodernism, or the Cultural Logic of Late Capitalism." *New Left Review* 146: 53-92.

Jauss, Hans Robert. 1982. *Toward an Aesthetic of Reception.* Minneapolis: University of Minnesota Press.

"Jerusalem Billboards Are Cultural Mosaic." 1992. *Chicago Tribune* February 9.

Kristof, Nicholas D. 1993. "Via Satellite, Information Revolution Stirs China." *New York Times* April 11.

Kroeber, Alfred L. and Kluckhohn, Clyde. 1952. *Culture: A Critical Review of Concepts and Definitions.* Cambridge, MA: Harvard University Peabody Museum of American Archeology and Ethnology.

Kunda, Gideon. 1992. *Engineering Culture: Control and Commitment in a High Tech Organization.* Philadelphia: Temple University Press.

Lamont, Michèle. 1992. *Money, Morals, and Manners: The Culture of the French and the American Upper-Middle Class.* Chicago: University of Chicago Press.

Lee, Leo Ou-fan and Nathan, Andrew J. 1985. "The Beginnings of Mass Culture: Journalism and Fiction in the Late Ch'ing and Beyond." In *Popular Culture in Late Imperial China.* David Johnson, Andrew J. Nathan, and Evelyn S. Rawski, eds. Berkeley: University of California Press. Pp. 360-395.

Lévi-Strauss, Claude. 1966. *The Savage Mind.* Chicago: University of Chicago Press.

Levine, Lawrence W. 1988. *Highbrow/Lowbrow: The Emergence of Cultural Hierarchy in America.* Cambridge, MA: Harvard University Press.

Liebes, Tamar and Katz, Elihu. 1990. *The Export of Meaning: Cross-Cultural Readings of Dallas*. New York: Oxford University Press.

Lincoln, James R. and Kalleberg, Arne L. 1990. *Culture, Control, and Commitment: A Study of Work Organizations and Work Attitudes in the United States and Japan*. Cambridge, UK: Cambridge University Press.

Link, E. Perry. 1992. *Evening Chats in Beijing: Probing China's Predicament*. New York: Norton.

Link, Perry. 1981. *Mandarin Ducks and Butterflies: Popular Fiction in Early Twentieth-Century China*. Berkeley: University of California Press.

Lippman, John. 1992. "Tuning In the Global Village." *Los Angeles Times* October 20.

Lowenthal, Leo. (1944) 1968. "The Triumph of Mass Idols." In *Literature, Popular Culture, and Society*. Palo Alto, CA: Pacific. Pp. 109-140.

Luker, Kristen. 1984. *Abortion and the Politics of Motherhood*. Berkeley: University of California Press.

Luker, Kristen. 1991. "Dubious Conceptions: The Controversy Over Teen Pregnancy." *The American Prospect* 5: 73-83.

Martin, Joanne. 1992. *Cultures in Organizations: Three Perspectives*. New York: Oxford University Press.

Martin, Joanne; Feldman, Martha S.; Hatch, Mary Jo; and Sitkin, Sim B. 1983. "The Uniqueness Paradox in Organizational Stories." *Administrative Science Quarterly* 28: 438-453.

Marx, Karl. 1977. "Preface to *A Critique of Political Economy*." In *Karl Marx: Selected Writings*. David McLellan, ed. Oxford: Oxford University Press. Pp. 388-392.

Marx, Karl and Engels, Frederick. 1970. *The German Ideology*. C. J. Arthur, ed. New York: International Publishers.

Maslow, Abraham H. 1962. *Toward a Psychology of Being*. New York: Van Nostrand.

Mead, George H. 1934. *Mind, Self, and Society From the Standpoint of a Social Behaviorist*. Chicago: University of Chicago Press.

Merton, Robert K. 1938. "Social Structure and Anomie." *American Sociological Review* 3: 672-682.

Meyer, John W. and Rowan, Brian. 1977. "Institutionalized Organizations: Formal Structure as Myth and Ceremony." *American Journal of Sociology* 83: 340-363.

Meyrowitz, Joshua. 1985. *No Sense of Place: The Impact of Electronic Media on Social Behavior*. New York: Oxford University Press.

Modleski, Tania. (1982) 1984. *Loving With a Vengeance: Mass-Produced Fantasies for Women*. New York: Methuen.

Neuhouser, Kevin. 1989. "Sources of Women's Power and Status Among the Urban Poor in Contemporary Brazil." *Signs* 14: 685-702.

Ogburn, William Fielding. (1922) 1936. *Social Change With Respect to Culture and Original Nature*. New York: Viking.

Okri, Ben. 1991. *The Famished Road*. London: Jonathan Cape.

Orrù, Marco; Biggart, Nicole Woolsey; and Hamilton, Gary G. 1991. "Organizational Isomorphism in East Asia." In *The New Institutionalism in Organizational Analysis*. Walter W. Powell and Paul J. DiMaggio, eds. Pp. 361-389.

Peterson, Richard A. 1978. "The Production of Cultural Change: The Case of Contemporary Country Music." *Social Forces* 45: 292-314.

Peterson, Richard A. 1979. "Revitalizing the Culture Concept." *Annual Review of Sociology* 5: 137-166.

Peterson, Richard A. 1992. "Understanding Audience Segmentation: From Elite and Mass to Omnivore and Univore." *Poetics* 21: 243-258.

Peterson, Richard A., ed. 1976. *The Production of Culture*. Beverly Hills, CA: Sage.

Powell, Walter W. and DiMaggio, Paul J. 1992. *The New Institutionalism in Organizational Analysis*. Chicago: University of Chicago Press.

Radway, Janice A. 1984. *Reading the Romance: Women, Patriarchy, and Popular Literature*. Chapel Hill: University of North Carolina Press.

Riesebrodt, Martin. 1993. *Pious Passion: The Emergence of Modern Fundamentalism in the United States and Iran*. Don Reneau, trans. Berkeley: University of California Press.

Rodriguez, Richard. 1982. *Hunger of Memory: The Education of Richard Rodriguez*. Boston: David Godine.

Sahlins, Marshall. 1985. *Islands of History*. Chicago: University of Chicago Press.

Scheper-Hughes, Nancy. 1992. *Death Without Weeping: The Violence of Everyday Life in Brazil*. Berkeley: University of California Press.

Shilts, Randy. 1987. *And the Band Played On: Politics, People, and the AIDS Epidemic*. New York: St. Martin's.

Snow, David A. and Anderson, Leon. 1993. *Down on Their Luck: A Study of Homeless Street People*. Berkeley: University of California Press.

Spence, Jonathan D. 1990. *The Search for Modern China*. New York: Norton.

Stendhal (Marie Henri Beyle). (1830) 1958. *The Red and the Black*. Lowell Bair, trans. New York: Bantam.

Stevens, Wallace. (1936) 1954. "The Man With the Blue Guitar." In *The Collected Poems of Wallace Stevens*. New York: Knopf. P. 165.

Swidler, Ann. 1986. "Culture in Action: Symbols and Strategies." *American Sociological Review* 51: 273-286.

Tannahill, Reay. 1973. *Food in History*. New York: Stein & Day.

Thomas, W. I. 1966. *On Social Organization and Social Personality*. Morris Janowitz, ed. Chicago: University of Chicago Press.

Tylor, Edward B. (1871) 1958. *Primitive Culture: Researches Into the Development of Mythology, Philosophy, Religion, Art, and Custom*. Gloucester, MA: Smith.

Watterson, Bill. 1988. *Something Under the Bed Is Drooling*. Kansas City, MO: Andrews & McMeel.

Weber, Max. (1904-5) 1958. *The Protestant Ethic and the Spirit of Capitalism*. Talcott Parsons, trans. New York: Scribner.

Weber, Max. 1946. "Science as a Vocation." In *From Max Weber: Essays in Sociology*. H. H. Gerth and C. Wright Mills, eds. New York: Oxford University Press. Pp. 129-156.

Webster's Third New International Dictionary. 1986. Springfield, MA: Merriam-Webster.

Wertham, Frederick. 1954. *Seduction of the Innocent*. New York: Rinehart.

White, Harrison C. and White, Cynthia A. 1965. *Canvases and Careers: Institutional Change in the French Painting World*. New York: John Wiley.

Williams, Raymond. (1973) 1980. "Base and Superstructure in Marxist Cultural Theory." In *Problems in Materialism and Culture*. London: Verso. Pp. 31-49.

Williams, Raymond. 1976. *Keywords: A Vocabulary of Culture and Society*. New York: Oxford University Press.

Willis, Paul. (1977) 1981. *Learning to Labor: How Working Class Kids Get Working Class Jobs*. New York: Columbia University Press.

Wilson, William Julius. 1987. *The Truly Disadvantaged: The Inner City, the Underclass, and Public Policy*. Chicago: University of Chicago Press.

Wolf, Arthur. 1974. "Ghosts, Gods, and Ancestors." In *Religion and Rituals in Chinese Society*. Stanford, CA: Stanford University Press.

Wuthnow, Robert. 1985. "State Structures and Ideological Outcomes." *American Sociological Review* 50: 799-821.

Wuthnow, Robert. 1987. *Meaning and Moral Order: Explorations in Cultural Analysis*. Berkeley: University of California Press.

Wuthnow, Robert and Witten, Marsha. 1988. "New Directions in the Study of Culture." *Annual Review of Sociology* 14: 49-67.

Yeats, William Butler. 1956. "The Second Coming." From *The Collected Poems of W. B. Yeats*. New York: Macmillan. P. 184.

Index